Aggression and Crimes of Violence

RECONSTRUCTION OF SOCIETY SERIES

General Editors

Robert E. Lana
Ralph L. Rosnow

AGGRESSION AND CRIMES OF VIOLENCE

Jeffrey H. Goldstein
Temple University

New York
Oxford University Press
1975

E03552

Selections from works by the following authors and publications were made possible by the kind permission of their respective publishers and representatives:

Richard Wright, *Black Boy*. Copyright 1937, 1942, 1944, 1945 by Richard Wright. By permission of Harper & Row, Publishers, Inc.

Albert Bandura, *Social Learning Theory*, p. 5. © 1971 by General Learning Corporation.

J. H. Goldstein, R. Davis, and D. Herman, in *Journal of Personality and Social Psychology*, 1975, 31, 162-70. Copyright 1975 by the American Psychological Association.

N. Morris and G. Hawkins, *The Honest Politician's Guide to Crime Control*. Copyright © 1970 by The University of Chicago Press.

Monica D. Blumenthal et al., *Justifying Violence: Attitudes of American Men*. © 1972. By permission of the authors and Survey Research Center, Institute for Social Research, the University of Michigan.

Oscar Newman, *Defensible Space: Crime Prevention through Urban Design*. Copyright © 1972 by Oscar Newman. By permission of Macmillan Publishing Co., Inc.

Karl Menninger, M.D., *The Crime of Punishment*. Copyright © 1966 by Jeannetta Lyle Menninger. By permission of the Viking Press, Inc.

J. F. Decker, in *Criminology*, Vol. 10, No. 2 (August 1972), p. 142. By permission of Sage Publications, Inc.

Ramsey Clark, *Crime in America*. © 1970 by Ramsey Clark. By permission of Simon & Schuster.

Richard Doan, The Doan Report in *TV Guide*. Copyright © 1974 by Triangle Publications, Inc. By permission of *TV Guide*® Magazine.

John Irwin, *The Felon*. © 1970. By permission of Prentice-Hall, Inc.

To the memory of my father, Robert

INTRODUCTION TO THE RECONSTRUCTION OF SOCIETY SERIES

When society requires to be rebuilt, there is no use in attempting to rebuild it on the old plan.

John Stuart Mill 1858

The problems of society are many and complex, and sound plans on which to rebuild it are few. Institutions that once seemed to work quite well, no longer do so; and many new programs, hastily conceived, have failed or just faded away into oblivion. Therefore, it is time now to reassess what has and has not been accomplished, to analyze and challenge our assumptions, and to offer new and more carefully conceived blueprints for rebuilding society.

That is the purpose of this book and of those which follow in this series, the Reconstruction of Society. We have asked knowledgeable social scientists to direct their theories and research toward solving some of the problems of society—to develop plans that are specific enough to be the basis for policy discussions and decisions. In the end, of course, even the best blueprint can be no more than a technical exercise if there is not the means and the will to bring it to fruition. Justice Felix Frankfurter once wrote: "In a democratic society like ours, relief must come through an aroused popular conscience that sears the conscience of the people's representatives." The ideas contained in the books in this series may be another step in that direction.

This, the first volume in the series, by Professor Jeffrey H. Goldstein, focuses upon one of the most distressing and perplexing problems in modern American society—the increase in violent crimes and the seeming escalation of aggressive behavior. Goldstein, a social psychologist, has written and done extensive field research in aggression. In this thoughtful and illuminating essay, he analyzes the basic nature of human aggression, and in the process dispels the myths and half-truths that abound. Coming to practical terms with the problem, he turns finally to the nature of our criminal justice system in the United States and proposes constructive alternatives for dealing more effectively with aggression and crimes of violence.

Robert E. Lana
Ralph L. Rosnow

Philadelphia, Pennsylvania
November, 1974

PREFACE

This book is intended to provide an overview of theory and research on *human* aggression which can serve as a foundation for the control and elimination of violence and violent crime. I emphasize human to indicate my belief that an understanding of so extraordinary and complex a species as man must ultimately come from a study of man himself. Both the scientific and popular literature on aggression are dominated by concern with infra-human species; I have tried to present a synthesis of research and theory pertaining directly to homo sapiens. In discussing human violence, I have generally ignored the traditional boundaries which separate scientists and their ideas from one another; the literature summarized in this book comes from a variety of disciplines, including anthropology, criminology, education, law, medicine, political science, psychiatry, psychology, sociology, and, on occasion, physiology. Since these diverse and sometimes divergent fields often use languages and concepts which are difficult to reconcile, a simple model of aggression is introduced in Chapter 1 which will provide a common language with which to evaluate and integrate these various approaches.

I have tried to write this book so as to make it accessible to nonpsychologists and students with no formal training in scientific methodology or statistics. In order to present a concise summary of the causes and possible solutions to crime and aggression, it has been necessary in some places to simplify the often complex and not entirely consistent research literature; where inconsistencies in the literature exist, I have pointed them out in footnotes. In other places, it has been necessary to fill gaps in our knowledge with hypothetical analyses which are subject to future test. I can only hope that my theoretical speculations will not be misconstrued as statements of fact. I have indicated in footnotes the sources for my statements as well as additional readings for those interested in pursuing a particular topic in greater depth.

Although the concept of aggression is examined critically in Chapter 1, an indication of how that term will be used is in order here. The definition of aggression used throughout this book is *behavior whose intent is the physical or psychological injury of another person.* Given this definition, not only hitting someone, but also embarrassing another person would be considered aggressive. Intentionally depriving another unnecessarily of some valued resource, such as a job, would also be aggressive. Obviously the crimes of homicide, assault, and rape are acts of aggression, but so too are the not illegal acts of spanking a child, name-calling, and nearly all forms of prejudice and discrimination. Excluded from this conception of aggression are accidental or unintentional injury of others as well as behaviors which, in popular parlance, are labeled aggressive simply because of their persistence or vigor, as in the term "aggressive salesman"; self-assertion is nonaggressive unless it is also designed to bring injury to another. The destruction of objects, as in smashing a vase against a wall, is likewise excluded from this conception of aggression because it does not involve injury to another human being. While it is possible to make a distinction between violence (the physical injury of others) and aggression (the psychological injury of others), the two terms are used interchangeably here. Although this definition of aggression will serve our purposes adequately, there are some difficulties associated with it, as others have indicated.[1] For example, there are some behaviors which are not clearly either aggressive or nonaggressive (such as euthanasia and abortion), and it is not always easy, or possible, to determine what a person's intentions were.

Aggression might best be viewed as a continuum in which any behavior can contain varying amounts of "aggressiveness." A behavior with no hostile intention to, but which nevertheless does injure another, would anchor one end of this dimension, while behavior solely designed to kill or permanently injure another would anchor the opposite end. Most behaviors of concern to us contain both aggressive and nonaggressive components. For example, throwing a punch at someone would be less aggressive than attempting to shoot him; spanking a child in order to "teach him a lesson" would be less aggressive than hitting him simply because one is having a "bad day." What has been referred to by psychologists as *instrumental aggression* (that is, aggressive behavior designed to achieve some particular goal, such as money) would, in this scheme, contain both aggressive and nonaggressive components, since the act is designed both to injure another as well as to produce a desired end-state for the aggressor. It is probably safe to say that most acts of aggression are in some ways also designed for a purpose other than the pure injury of another. One of the main contentions of this book is that aggressive behavior used by someone to achieve a personal goal, such as wealth or power, and which may be perceived by the actor as justified (or even as nonaggressive) is a primary cause of the aggressive and criminal behavior of others. Wars are always fought for the greater good, but they beget, among other things, future wars.

1. H. Kaufmann. *Aggression and altruism.* N. Y.: Holt, Rinehart & Winston, 1970. J. T. Tedeschi, R. B. Smith, III., & R. C. Brown, Jr. A reconceptualization of aggression. Unpublished manuscript, State Univ. of New York, Albany.

There are several reasons why I have chosen to write this book. The first has to do with what I see as the recent overemphasis which has been placed on biological determinants of aggression. In order to counterbalance this viewpoint, I have stressed social and environmental causes of aggression. The rationale for such an approach is presented in Chapter 1. Second, I have tried to incorporate ideas and research from a number of scientific disciplines in order to demonstrate that, while aggression is often spoken of in different terms by those in different specialties, their various approaches to and conceptualizations of aggression often have much in common. While my own training, and therefore the emphasis of the book, is psychological, the ideas incorporated within it derive from a variety of fields. Third, I have tried to demonstrate that the violence which appalls so many people today—muggings, robberies, rapes, murders—is not so very different from the aggression in which most people engage on a less grand scale. The difference between a "criminal" and a "noncriminal" is not qualitative, but a matter of degree.

Although the technical literature on aggression and crime is voluminous, only a minute portion of it is addressed to potential solutions to these problems. There are several reasons why this is so. First, scientists have been reluctant to speak on social issues *as scientists* because they are aware of the uncertainties inherent in all scientific endeavors; scientific statements are probabilistic and not absolute. Second, it is impossible to discuss remedies for violence with great confidence unless one also has confidence that he understands the conditions which bring about violence. Because scientists are prone to basing conclusions on empirical research, they seem to be awaiting more research before addressing themselves to solutions. But research is not a process with a finite end; there is *always* the need for more research. I have therefore proposed a number of solutions to the problems of crime and violence based on the research and theory currently available. In this sense, the proposed solutions presented in Chapters 5 and 6 must be considered tentative. I would urge that the hypotheses underlying proposed remedies be tested before the remedies are instituted on any large scale. To this end, the criminal-legal enterprise should itself become an experimenting body in order to determine which of several alternative strategies for the control of aggression and crime are most likely to succeed.

To provide a basis for arriving at plausible solutions to the problems of aggression and violent crime, I have made some preliminary analyses in Chapters 2 through 4 and have arrived at hypotheses based on these analyses. I present them throughout this book as precisely what they are—tentative statements which cannot be accepted as "true" in the absence of supportive research. In making recommendations for the control and elimination of violence, I will assume that these hypotheses are likely to be supported; if time proves a hypothesis false, then naturally the suggested remedies based on that hypothesis will have to be modified accordingly. Even if a hypothesis were consistently supported by research data, there would always be some danger in generalizing to statements of policy, statements of what "ought" to be. I would be the last to argue that systems of socialization and criminal justice should be based *exclusively* on findings from the behavioral sciences. Certainly there are other than scientific considerations involved in issues of criminal justice, child-rearing, interpersonal and international relations. I would argue, however, that wherever possible, research findings be taken into consideration and that policy decisions not contradict scientific research and theory unless the possible consequences of such a contradiction are known and weighed.

Since I have defined aggression as the intentional injury of another person, I have no compunction about treating it in the pages which follow as an undesirable feature of human behavior. Although it may be possible in some circumstances to justify aggression, I see it as the least desirable means of resolving interpersonal and intergroup disputes and conflicts.

While writing this book I have been the recipient of the wisdom, counsel and support of good friends and colleagues. My greatest debt is to Frank Winer, who has painstakingly read and commented on the entire manuscript. I have also been the beneficiary of advice and suggestions on portions of the manuscript from James Averill, Ronald Baenninger, Helene Feinberg, Robert Feinberg, James Hurley, David Kipnis, George Levinger, Ashley Montagu, Jack Rakosky, and Harriet Serenkin. While I am pleased to acknowledge their contributions to this book, I must at the same time absolve them of any responsibility for the errors, ambiguities, and inconsistencies which may remain. Temple University kindly consented to my request for a study leave, and the University of Massachusetts, Amherst, generously provided the facilities and the ambience in which to write this book. Portions of the book were written with the support of a grant from Temple University and with a National Science Foundation grant to the Department of Psychology, University of Massachusetts.

J. H. G.
Amherst, Mass.
July 1974

CONTENTS

Aggression and Crimes of Violence

THE NATURE OF HUMAN AGGRESSION

1

The views we hold about why people commit crimes deeply influence our ways of dealing with them.

Leon Radzinowicz[1]

Most of us are familiar with acts of aggression, either through personal experience or through the mass media. A report in the July 11, 1973, *New York Times* indicated that 34 per cent of adult women in one congressional district of New York City were the victims of serious crimes in 1972. Even if we have not been so victimized, we may have engaged in hitting our children or spouse or have seen combat on the battlefields of Korea, Vietnam, Harlem, or Watts. Or we may have been involved in less direct, though no less damaging acts of aggression, as in refusing food to someone hungry or failing to try to stop a fight — or a war. In the pages to follow, various aspects common to these examples of aggression will be explored and possible causes and remedies will be examined.

In order to begin the journey toward the examination of the diverse behaviors called aggression, several fundamental issues must first be discussed. Foremost among these is the heritability of aggression: Is man doomed by his genes to slaughter his neighbor?

IS AGGRESSION AN INSTINCT?

Throughout modern history the answer to the question of whether aggression is innate or learned has swung first toward one pole and then the other. Because at various times the answer to the question has changed, there are in our social and judicial systems techniques and remedies for the reduction and control of violence which are not necessarily consistent with one another nor with current scientific thinking on the issue. The point I wish to make is not that scientific thinking changes over time—it should and does change as new information is acquired—but that the formal and informal policies and controls which are used to reduce aggression are influenced by whether aggression is conceived of as innate or learned.

Mid-twentieth-century thinking leans toward the instinctual pole due to three major influences: the very readable accounts of aggression by ethologists Konrad Lorenz, and Desmond Morris, and Robert Ardrey;[2] the popularity and pervasiveness of Freudian theory;[3] and the dramatic research on electrical and chemical stimulation of the brain.[4]

One Giant Leap Toward Mankind

The ethological arguments proposed by Lorenz, Morris and Ardrey can be summarized by saying that there is ample evidence that our animal ancestors were instinctively violent beings, and since we have evolved from them, we too must be the bearers of destructive impulses in our genetic composition. Lorenz states, "There cannot be any doubt, in the opinion of any biologically minded scientist, that intraspecific aggression is, in man, just as much of a spontaneous instinctive drive as in most other higher vertebrates."[5]

There are essentially two difficulties with this argument. First, the evidence that animals, at least the higher primates, are instinctively aggressive is not at all convincing. Binford has examined the evidence and found it seriously wanting, as have Alland, Montagu, Schneirla, and Scott.[6] Second, even if the evidence reviewed by Lorenz, Morris, and Ardrey were sufficient to warrant the conclusion that infrahuman species were innately violent, we would still have to ask whether that proves anything at all about proneness to aggression in man. The answer, of course, is that it does not. The *likelihood* that man is instinctively aggressive would be increased if all animals were shown conclusively to be aggressive, but we would still have to entertain the possibility that homo sapiens, having evolved as an independent species, was not.

I should like to point out that research on animals can serve as a valuable tool in the study of human behavior. It does *not necessarily* tell us anything about humans, but it can serve as a valuable source of ideas and hypotheses to be tested using human research subjects. I would be reluctant to take a new drug which had not first been tested successfully on animals. But such tests would not insure that the drug would have the same effects upon me as it did on the animal test subjects.

There is not much doubt that man *can* behave like phylogenetically inferior species. There is no reason whatever why an organism with a complex nervous system, such as man, cannot behave like or mimic, if you will, the behavior of animals with less complex nervous systems. But to argue that, because man *can* behave like lower organisms, this is the way he *must* behave is simply fallacious. If we take learning experiments on animals, particularly those operant conditioning studies in which an organism is rewarded for performing a certain response, there is no neurological or psychological reason why a human being cannot also learn responses in this way. But to argue that this is *the* way that humans learn—simply because it is *one* way in which they may learn—is begging the question. It is obviously true that human beings can and do learn behaviors through operant conditioning. However, to preclude other uniquely human ways of learning is a serious shortcoming of much contemporary psychology. Likewise, to argue that man learns aggression in the same ways that animals learn aggression (if indeed it is learned in animals) is to ignore the rather likely possibility that there are species-specific aggressions in man or that there are specifically human routes to learning and behaving.

Monkeying Around in the Brains of Primates

Research on brain physiology and chemistry, particularly that on electrical and chemical stimulation of the brain, has demonstrated that it is possible in many instances to make normally docile animals—and humans—extraordinarily violent. The best known work in this field has been done by José Delgado[7] at Yale. By implanting sensitive radio receivers in various parts of the brain of cats, monkeys, and other species, Delgado has been able to control the aggressive behavior of his research subjects by activating various parts of the limbic system, particularly the hypothalamus. Heath[8] has reported a similar ability to control aggression in humans.

What implications does this dramatic research hold for an understanding of, and ability to control, human aggression? First, and perhaps most important, is the frightening possibility that human aggressiveness could be controlled by others against the actor's will. Electrodes could be implanted in infants' brains at birth, or in adults' during routine operations, without the knowledge or consent of the recipients. Aggression could then be fairly reliably controlled by the possessor of the appropriate radio transmitter. Both Moyer and Clark[9] have made elegant appeals that such technological abilities not be used for antisocial purposes, if indeed they are used at all.

In many of the brain stimulation studies on aggression, it has been reported that, even when stimulated, some animals will not engage in aggression unless certain environmental features are present, such as an "appropriate" target for attack.[10] Thus, even with infrahumans, brain stimulation does not guarantee that aggression will ensue, a finding which calls into question the notion that aggression is purely a matter of brain chemistry and physiology, as some have argued.[11] Let us suppose, however, that the research discussed here was even more conclusive, that by stimulating the brain's lateral hypothalamus aggression could be uniformly and consistently elicited from men as well as from animals. The evidence is far from this reliable, but if it were, what would this mean insofar as our ability to understand, predict, and control human aggression was concerned? My own conclusion would be that it has very little demonstrable relevance. While the brain stimulation research has now been conducted in a sufficient number of circumstances to prove of some generality, it says nothing about how the brain is stimulated in vivo. What are those variables which cause the lateral hypothalamus to be stimulated when an organism's skull remains intact? One answer, of course, is that changes in body chemistry are likely to suppress or activate different parts of the hypothalamus, but the question of what variables influence what hormones to activate the hypothalamus remains largely unexplored. It is likely that stimuli residing outside the person, in his or her environment, are those that influence body chemistry. We will have to look outside the corporal package, then, in order to answer this question satisfactorily.

As with research on infrahuman species, physiological research can provide us with valuable information about the nature of aggression mechanisms. It has instructed us within a very short period of time and within fairly narrow limits which internal structures are likely to be implicated in aggressive behavior. However, physiology is only one part of the complex problem of aggression. That aggression is a physical act there can be no doubt, and that brain physiology and chemistry are involved in aggressive behavior is equally clear. Environmental and cognitive factors, though, are also implicated in the physiological research. Stimulation of parts of the brain does not guarantee that aggressive behavior will ensue, and, further, it is likely that in natural situations (i.e., those of nonintervention in the brain) it is mental or cognitive and environmental factors that are themselves responsible for the stimulation in the first place. It is also conceivable that those portions of the brain found during surgical intervention to elicit aggression are not those involved in nonintervention situations. Though I think this an unlikely possibility, it does serve to point out the difficulties in generalizing from a contrived to a natural situation.

"Born to Raise Hell"   One aspect of the physiology of aggression deserves mention in view of its having received a good deal of publicity and because it indicates what may be a close relationship between aggressive and sexual behavior, the "XYY Syndrome."* The normal male has, as one of his 23 pairs of chromosomes, one pair which determine sex characteristics, an X and a Y chromosome (the normal female has two X chromosomes). Occasionally, males have an extra Y chromosome. The incidence of XYY males in the population is approximately 1 in 3000.

Several studies have reported that, among persons institutionalized for violent behavior, the incidence of XYY males far exceeds their proportion in the total population. Jacobs and coworkers[12] estimated that 3 per cent of the men in maximum security prisons and hospitals for the "criminally insane" in Edinburgh were XYY's. We must be cautious in drawing conclusions from this kind of data. Over 95 per cent of those incarcerated for violence were not XYY males, and it is unlikely that all XYY males showed signs of excessive violence. If the XYY Syndrome is a cause of violence, it is only a contributory one which requires other conditions for aggression to occur and, in any event, is capable of accounting for only a small proportion of total violence.[13]

If our concern were to predict, for any given individual, the

---

* Ashley Montagu points out that the XYY phenomenon is not a syndrome which reliably leads to particular behaviors, but an anomaly which, depending upon environmental circumstances, may lead to a wide variety of possible behaviors. See his "Chromosomes and Crime," *Psychology Today,* October 1968, 42-49.

probability that he would behave violently, we would have to predict that an XYY male would more probably be aggressive than a normal XY male and that the possession of certain brain abnormalities would also increase the probability of aggression. But these increased probabilities should not be confused with linear and direct causality. As any student of science knows, a correlation between two events does not mean that one causes the other. Let us assume, for example, that the majority of violent crimes are committed by the poor against the poor. This does not mean that lack of material wealth causes crime. If we were to deprive a millionaire of his money, it is unlikely that he would suddenly become a violent criminal, and if we were to provide unlimited wealth to a violent criminal, it is unlikely that he would disengage himself from his violent ways. There are undoubtedly other factors associated with poverty which are the actual causes of violence, not poverty itself.*

Freudian Slips

Although Freud initially proposed that there was only one instinctive force motivating human behavior, the *life instinct* or Eros, his inability to explain the horrors of a world war with this positive instinct led him to modify his theory and add to it a second instinctive force, Thanatos or the *death instinct*. Freud suggested that societies must learn to control the expression of both the life and death instincts. Thus are developed social mores and rules regulating sexual and aggressive conduct. Violation of these rules is usually punishable under the laws of the society.

---

* A possible reconciliation between the social psychological approach taken in this book and the physiological approach to aggression is quite feasible. It is conceivable that those centers of the brain which are capable of evoking aggression are located entirely or primarily in the older and more primitive portions of the brain, the paleocortex, while those centers responsible for the inhibition of aggression and for nonaggressive responses are located in the more recently evolved brain centers, the neocortex. We could then view the conflicts around which aggression revolves in physiological as well as in social and psychological terms.

Contemporary psychoanalytic theorists, building more or less on Freud's own work, have retained the notion that aggression is an instinctive drive. Common in current psychoanalytic thinking is the notion that aggression must be discharged periodically lest it build up to such a point that its expression becomes spontaneous and uncontrollable. Zinberg and Fellman[14] go so far as to suggest that war itself serves to discharge the aggression instinct not only for the participants but for the civilian "spectators" as well. They say that "a mature society . . . must eventually accept violence as an essential part of human nature, essential not because it is good or bad but essential because it is there" (p. 540). Likewise, Storr and May discuss ways by which aggression can be acceptably discharged before it reaches a dangerous level, and Glover states that "crime is part of the price paid for the domestication of a naturally wild animal (man)" (p. 7).[15]

Of importance here is the notion that aggression is an instinctive behavior; that, if it is not regularly expressed it will build up to a dangerously high level which can then lead to excessive and spontaneous discharge; and that it is possible to vicariously reduce aggression by observing violence in others, a process known as *catharsis*. There is one other aspect of current psychoanalytic theory which also deserves mention. According to various psychoanalytical theories it is possible that a person can invoke one or more of several "ego defense mechanisms" to prevent the expression of aggressive drives. (This is also said of sexual instincts where sexual energy can be denied expression and used in other endeavors, a process known as *sublimation*.) Aggressive energy can be channeled into nonaggressive behaviors, according to Freudian theories. Thus, it is postulated that (a) all people have aggression instincts but (b) not everyone will behave aggressively, owing to the use of various defense mechanisms. This kind of internal ambiguity makes psychoanalytic theories extraordinarily difficult to test in a scientific fashion, and it is largely for this reason—that almost any research finding can be interpreted as support for the theory—that it is

still considered viable by many. With regard to those parts of
the theory which are testable, such as the notions that aggression
regularly and inevitably increases with the passage of time and
that aggression can be discharged vicariously, almost all have
been generally unsupported by research.[16]

In the Minds of Men

From this point forward, I will deal with human aggression except in those instances in which animal data may serve as a useful source of hypotheses to be tested with human research subjects. In terms of the flexibility of behavior, contemporary
psychologists often speak as though human, like much animal,
aggression is highly stereotypic, consisting of characteristic
forms of expression. Anthropologists have known for some time
that human aggression—if it is present in a society at all—can
be expressed in a wide variety of ways, and that these particular
forms of expression are learned. As early as 1939, Boring, Langfeld and Weld[17] could say:

> . . . conflict between individuals does not invariably or uni-
> versally result in the same behavior. Instead of fighting with
> his fists, the Kwakiutl Indian fights with property in the in-
> stitution of the "potlatch," in which the more property he can
> give away or destroy, the more superior he is to his opponent.
> Eskimos settle their conflicts in a public contest in which each
> sings abusive songs about the other. When two Indians of
> Santa Marta quarrel, instead of striking each other they strike
> a tree or rock with sticks, and the one first breaking his stick
> is considered the braver and hence the victor. In other societies
> aggression is expressed in still other ways; even within the same
> society there may be a wide range of different socially approved
> expressions of aggression (p. 163).

More recently, Goode[18] has argued:

> That few men do kill or maim others seems to refute the notion
> of a biological urge or instinct to murder. Whatever man's ag-

gressive impulses, obviously most men learn to control them. Much more compelling, however, are the great differences in homicide and assault rates among nations, regions within nations, (e.g., the southern United States or Italy as compared with the north), classes and ethnic groups, the two sexes. The differences are so great as not to be explicable, except by reference to *social* factors.

If we examine aggression in different cultures we find little evidence that it is universal. Of course, all that needs to be done to refute the hypothesis that aggression is a universal instinct is to point to those societies which show no overt signs of violence, such as the Arapesh, the Lepchas, and the pygmies of the Ituri rain forest.[19] Most recently, the Tasaday of the Philippine Islands have been studied by a small team of researchers who report no evidence of overt hostility among them. There have been few enough "Appollonian" peoples, as Ruth Benedict has called members of nonviolent cultures, so that it could be argued that the nonaggressive cultures are in some sense merely mutations, exceptions which prove the rule that homo sapiens is innately aggressive. After all, the Tasaday, the Arapesh of New Guinea, the Lepchas of Sikkim, and the Ituri pygmies of the Congo constitute only a small portion of humanity. I do not think that this is the case, however. In the absence of positive evidence that these groups are genetically atypical, I conclude that the existence of such nonviolent peoples indicates that humans are not necessarily aggressive.

Neither the evidence from animal or psychophysiological research nor from psychoanalytic and anthropological research justifies the conclusion that as a species we are all the carriers of violent impulses which are bound to expression. Why, then, the recurrent and strongly held belief that aggression will out? Binford recounts several reasons why such beliefs have become widespread among nonscientists, for example, our need to expiate guilt while involved in the Vietnam war. But to account for their popularity among scientists, we must go beyond her statement. While scientists, no less than others, would like to alleviate feelings of personal responsibility for the state of the world, there are additional reasons why not a few scientists tend to adhere to such views. First, aggression and violence are most difficult phenomena to study scientifically; sound methodology in research is difficult to achieve since it is both unethical and problematic to engage human research subjects in acts of violence. Therefore, in the absence of sound research, theoretical development suffers. Since theory on the origins of aggression must then be relatively weak, scientists tend to take the path of least resistance and ascribe aggression to biological necessity. The problem thus "explained" frees the scientist to research more accessible problems. (Freud, for example, initially attempted to explain the presence of human aggression in terms of the life instinct, but he could not explain the horrors of war in such terms and so proposed an aggression instinct. Things then became more readily "understandable.") A second reason for scientists' attraction to instinctual theories of aggression is that the variety and prevalence of aggressive phenomena defy simple, one-dimensional explanations. If one tries to account for aggression in purely sociological terms, such as social class and status deprivation, there are counterexamples which cannot easily be fit within the theory. For example, some have argued that aggression is found most often among those who are poor, powerless, and alienated from the mainstream of society; but they immediately encounter the fact that *most* people who are poor, powerless, and alienated are not aggressive (even though most aggressive acts may be committed by people who fit such a description). Clearly an additional factor must be invoked to account for why only some poor and powerless people are aggressive while others, the majority, are not. This factor has so far eluded sociologists. Likewise, to account for aggression in terms of learning, psychologists run into counterexamples, in which those who live among aggressive people, who are encouraged to be aggressive, and who are recipients of rewards for their aggression, will not necessarily lead lives of violence. Physiologists and biologists who view aggression as a function of neurological and brain damage encounter people who suffer from brain damage without being aggressive and people who are aggressive but who suffer no brain damage. Counterexamples, of course, do not indicate that any of these approaches is fully incorrect; they indicate that these theories are at best too simple to provide adequate explanations. Since it is scientifically desirable to arrive at the simplest theory possible which is consistent with the facts, scientists often resort to the simplest of all possible theories, that people behave the way they do because it is genetically programmed into them.

A major objection to the notion of instinct is that it is not subject to empirical test; there is no ethical way to empirically prove that any complex behavior is an instinct in humans. In recent years, even animal researchers have softened their notion of what an instinct is. No longer is an instinct believed to be a purely internal impulse to engage in certain behavior. In most circumstances external environmental requirements must also be met before an "instinct" is expressed. Tinbergen[20] has suggested that instinct be replaced by the term *fixed-action pattern* to indicate that the behavior is not spontaneously emitted by the organism, but is most typically elicited by external stimulation in conjunction with some internal state of the organism.

One rule of science is to assume that nothing is "true" unless the evidence indicates that it is not false; to accept the *null hypothesis* unless there is sufficient reason to reject it. Therefore, it behooves us to reject the aggressive instinct hypothesis as insufficiently supported by the evidence; if not to reject it, at least to hold it in abeyance until more definitive evidence is compiled. We can start with the hypothesis that man is a tabula rasa at birth; that he is neither predisposed toward aggression nor passivity, and that what he becomes is a product of what happens to him and where. Of course, man is not "nothing" at birth, but is a complex bundle of physiological, genetic, and corporal baggage which set limits on both what and how he can learn and predispose him to learn certain things more readily than others. The infant is potentially many people (though not an infinite number) and the person the infant becomes is determined by the environment in which it is reared and by the specific events which transpire in its life. Thus, we will assume that aggression is learned, but learning here takes on a broad meaning and extends beyond the bounds of what psychologists traditionally mean by "learning theory." It is safe to say that we are all born with the *capacity and potential* for learning to behave violently. After all, we are capable of using our hands, feet, and teeth to punch, kick, and bite anyone or anything we choose. We are capable of designing and making weapons for destruction, and it can be argued convincingly that these potentialities are inherited as part of our corporal structures. In these ways, we are all potentially aggressive. To argue, however, that we instinctually use our hands, feet, teeth, and tool-making ability to inflict damage on our fellow man is, as can be seen from the evidence reviewed above, quite at variance with scientific reality.

THE UNITY OF HUMAN AGGRESSION

When confronted with a large and diverse set of elements one way to simplify and make some sense of them is to "type" them by sorting them into categories (usually with a large pile reserved for "miscellaneous"). Students of human aggression have often attempted to reduce the complex and quite varied acts of aggression in which men have engaged by subdividing aggression into various types and then proceeding to explore one or more of these types. However, in the absence of any sufficient reason for parsing aggressive behavior, we ought to begin with the assumption that aggression is a uniform behavior; that the factors which underlie and determine one act of aggression are also those which determine other acts.

Historically, there have been three bases which have led scholars to categorize aggressive acts into subtypes—theoretical, empirical, and legal. Theoretical bases for dividing violence into various types generally stem from the fact that different theories are capable of explaining and predicting only limited instances of aggression, and so theorists have divided aggression into types depending upon their ease of explanation. Empirical bases for categorizing aggression stem from the fact that different acts of aggression have, or seem to have, either different antecedent conditions or different amounts of force, premeditation, or emotional arousal involved. Thus, distinctions are often made by social psychologists between "angry" aggression, which assumes the actor to be emotionally excited immediately prior to his aggressive act, and "nonangry" aggressive behavior.[21] The target of aggression has also been used as a basis for distinguishing types of violence. According to the frustration–aggression theory, first proposed in 1939 by Dollard, Doob, Miller, Mowrer, and Sears,[22] aggression can be displaced onto a target other than the frustrator in an act of "displaced aggression." Attacking the initial frustrator would be an example of "direct aggression." The means and amount of activity involved in an act have been used by Buss[23] to categorize aggression. Buss' typology is presented in Table 1-1. All of the "active" varieties of aggression clearly fit within our definition of aggression; they all involve the intentional delivery of physical or psychological injury to

TABLE 1.1

A typology of human aggressive behaviors

	Active		Passive	
	Direct	Indirect	Direct	Indirect
Physical	Punching the victim	Practical joke; booby trap	Obstructing passage; sit-in	Refusing to perform a necessary task
Verbal	Insulting the victim	Malicious gossip	Refusing to speak	Refusing consent, vocal or written

Adapted from Buss, p. 8. By permission of author and publisher.

another. The passive varieties are also designed to cause psychological injury to others and, therefore, also meet our criteria for aggression. Whether or not such distinctions have any bearing on our interpretation and explanation of violence remains to be seen.

Moyer[24] has categorized animal aggression into several types, depending upon the physiological mechanisms involved in the aggression and the conditions under which the behavior is displayed. But even these types of animal aggression are not found in all species, and there is no a priori reason to expect all of them to be present in homo sapiens. Furthermore, human behavior is considerably more modifiable by experience and learning than lower organisms', and so humans are unlikely to respond "automatically" to any internal or external set of conditions.

American and English law also make distinctions between kinds or degrees of violence. Some violence is perfectly legal, but legal violence has its bounds. While it is legal to physically punish a child, it is illegal to batter a child. The distinction is only one of degree, and the law is not very precise on the dividing line. Illegal acts of violence may be categorized on the basis of victim, forethought, intentionality, means, or age of the aggressor. Aggressive acts committed by juveniles are distinguished from those committed by adults; acts involving a law enforcement officer or federal agents as victims are often distinguished from those involving private citizens; acts which are premeditated are legally distinct from those which are "spontaneous"; acts committed while engaged in another crime, such as a felony, are seen as legally distinct from those not so committed; and violence which is intentional is legally different from that which is accidental. The law also allows for acts committed while the actor was in some way unable to exert cognitive, rational control over his or her own behavior, such as violence committed in the heat of passion or while "temporarily insane."

What are we to make of these various characterizations of aggression? Since our goals in this book are to provide explanations for aggression and means to control and eliminate violence, we will have to approach this problem from the perspective of these aims. We have seen in the preceding pages that several factors may serve as contributory causes of aggressive behavior, such as electrical brain stimulation and the XYY Syndrome. It is conceivable, though it has by no means been proven, that individuals with certain genetic or organic disorders may be violence prone. Such people, whose violence is beyond their desire or control, would be excluded from the present analysis since it is questionable whether their behavior has the intention necessary to qualify as aggression. Nevertheless, even if their aggressive behavior is not designed to injure others in any conscious way, their actions are certainly destructive of others and would be considered aggressive by most observers. For the purposes of our analysis, however, we will exclude organic disorders since it is unlikely that those who suffer from them aggress with the conscious intention of injuring others.

Much aggressive and destructive behavior is only tangential to some other behavior. Most policemen who are killed while on duty are shot by people intent only on avoiding arrest for some other crime; their immediate intention is not the injury of a policeman, but the avoidance of arrest. Nevertheless, we would have to consider such behavior to be within the realm of our definition of aggression since there can be little doubt in the actor's mind that shooting a gun at someone is likely to injure or kill the person. Even though the aggressor's immediate intention is not the injury of the policeman, his actions while bent on escape are designed to injure and, therefore, even though his behavior is what many would call "instrumental" (that is, designed to achieve some end other than the injury of another) it is nonetheless aggressive. The distinction between an aggressor with a genetic or neurological disorder, which in some sense impels him to violence, and a felon acting to avoid apprehension, is a psychological or cognitive one. In the former case, the actor does not have the ability to aggress or not aggress, he "must" behave as he does, while in the latter case, choice is present. It is the ability to choose—to intend—which makes the felon's behavior aggressive.

A GENERAL MODEL OF AGGRESSION

In order to provide some structure and continuity to the discussions which follow, a simple model of aggressive behavior is presented here which will serve as a guideline in examining various instances of human aggression. Aggressive behavior is a complex act, based on a number of simultaneously acting factors. In order for aggression to occur, there must be some impetus to aggress, inhibitions against aggressing must be overcome, and the situation—in terms of the opportunity and ability to aggress and the availability of a target—must be appropriate. Given these aspects of every act of violence, any model of aggressive behavior will have to incorporate these factors within it.

It is proposed here that two sets of opposing tendencies operate in any potentially aggressive situation: tendencies to aggress and tendencies not to aggress.[25] The aggression expressed is a product of this conflict. The decision of whether or not to aggress in any particular situation depends upon the relative strength of these two opposing tendencies. When the number and strength of all the pro-aggression factors outweigh the number and strength of the anti-aggression factors, aggression will ensue. When the anti-aggression factors are stronger than the pro-aggression forces, no aggression will result.

We can divide the pro- and anti-aggression factors into long-term factors and situational factors. *Long-term* factors are those which are relatively enduring, or personality characteristics of the individual, such as his or her norms, attitudes, and values toward aggression, prior experiences with aggression, and knowledge of and ability to use aggressive or nonaggressive strategies in interpersonal disputes. Likewise, in any given instance, there are situational idiosyncrasies which may facilitate or inhibit aggressive behavior. These immediate, *situational factors* often play a prominent role in any act of violence. Although subse-

quent chapters are devoted to these four components—long-term
and situational factors associated with tendencies to aggress and
with tendencies not to aggress—a brief discussion of each will
be given for the sake of clarity.

Long-Term Factors Facilitating Aggression

The primary source of enduring factors toward aggression is the
socialization of the child. During socialization, the child acquires
a set of values, norms, attitudes, beliefs, and expectations about
aggressive behavior. These long-term norms[26] are usually acquired through selective reinforcements from, and the examples
set by, one's parents, peers, and teachers. Although no two individuals are apt to share identical norms about the appropriateness, means, or desirability for aggression, large groups, such
as whole societies or subcultures within any society, are likely
to have many norms in common.[27] For example, most Americans learn that aggression is desirable when used in defense of
country, self, personal property, or the law.

These long-term norms, once acquired by an individual, are
relatively stable and are likely to remain unchanged during one's
lifetime. Two reasons can be given for the persistence of such
norms. First, the individual is likely to have continued contact
with others who share his or her norms and with those from
whom he or she acquired them initially. A considerable body
of evidence indicates that people are most likely to be attracted
to others who share their basic attitudes, values, and norms.[28]
Second, once norms are acquired, one's subsequent experiences
and beliefs are organized around and integrated within one's
existing normative framework. Basic norms and values, then,
become the bulwark of subsequent beliefs and experiences.

Norms are acquired through processes of experience, modeling, and conditioning, and the agents of such learning include
parents, peers, and teachers, as well as informal social agents,
such as symbolic figures of authority as depicted in books, newspapers, movies, and television. In the next chapter we will examine such learning processes.

Situational Factors Facilitating Aggression

Given that an individual may have positive norms toward aggression, it is still the case that even the most violent individual is not perpetually violent, and even the most passive among us is likely to be instigated to aggression under certain circumstances. The circumstances which facilitate aggression are considered under the heading of situational factors. Among such factors are those which diminish normal inhibitions against aggressing, such as familiar environments, the presence of friends and relatives, victims associated in the actor's mind with aggression, and alcohol. Other situational factors discussed in Chapter 3 are the presence and availability of a weapon, emotional arousal and frustration, and physical environments which facilitate anonymity of the actor and his actions. Any factor which momentarily raises one's tendencies to aggress or lowers one's restraints against aggressing will be considered as a situational pro-aggression factor.

Long-Term Factors Facilitating Nonaggression

At the same time that people learn which situations, targets, and means are appropriate for aggression, they also learn which situations, targets, and means are inappropriate. In our society, we tend to learn that certain people are inappropriate targets of violence, such as women, the aged, and young children. We learn which specific behaviors are admissible in a fight and which behaviors are taboo; which situations are "aggressible" and which are not. *Aggressible situations* would include barrooms, public streets, vacant lots; *nonaggressible locations* include other peoples' homes, theaters, churches. Although these informal rules are sometimes broken, people in general are less likely to aggress in nonaggressible than in aggressible situations and are less likely to attack victims who are not deemed to be acceptable targets for aggression rather than those who are. Given these informal and generally recognized rules, we would have to conclude that an actor who aggresses against an old woman in a church would be acting more aggressively (in the sense that he has violated more taboos or overcome more resistance) than one who engaged in precisely the same physical acts against a thirty year old man in a barroom.

One reason for treating pro- and anti-aggression systems independently is to stress that there may be factors which encourage nonaggressive behavior which are not simply the absence of factors which encourage aggression. In other words, people may learn positive forms of social intercourse rather than mere inactivity as an alternative to violence.[29] One person may deal with interpersonal conflict by being nonaggressive because of the fear of the consequences for acting aggressively, while another may act nonaggressively because of the belief that disputes ought to be resolved by verbal arbitration. Thus, not acting aggressively does not mean precisely the same thing as acting nonaggressively.

Situational Factors Facilitating Nonaggression

Even the most violent people tend to be nonviolent in many, perhaps most, circumstances. The situational factors which are likely to reduce aggression are the presence of a potentially punishing agent, such as a parent or policeman, an unfamiliar environment, unfamiliar potential victims, easy identifiability of the actor and his actions, a strong sense of individuality or self, and the presence of nonaggressive others. These and related factors are discussed in Chapter 4.

How do these four sets of actors combine to determine aggression? Since aggression is viewed as the result of a conflict, the probability of aggressive behavior is given by the ratio of pro-aggression elements, both situational and long-term, to anti-aggressive elements, situational as well as long-term. (See page 88.)

Each of the factors in the model can be perceived as more or less important by different people or by the same person at different times. Thus, it is implied by the model that aggression conflict is based not only on the simple sum of pro- and anti-aggression factors but also on their relative importance to the individual involved. According to the model, one reason that aggression occurs is because a variety of norms and values may be in conflict with one another. It should be noted that this is quite a different notion than the one proposed by a number of sociologists (most notably Emile Durkheim) who view aggression and antisocial behavior to be the result of too few norms (a state referred to as *anomie*).

The model is essentially a conflict model, and several immediate consequences of this fact should be indicated. First, the behavior (aggressive or nonaggressive) engaged in by an individual in an interpersonal situation is the result of a number of factors. Second, the relationship of any single element to aggression will depend upon the number and type of other elements present, both as part of the individual's personality as well as the situation in which the individual finds oneself. Third, in viewing aggression as the result of a cognitive or mental conflict, we would expect the act of aggression to have cognitive consequences. As we shall see in Chapter 3, aggressive behavior (and nonaggressive behavior as well) has reliable cognitive effects, among which are re-evaluation of the social situation, of the victim, and of the conflict. Fourth, since the number of pro- and anti-aggression elements in any given situation may vary from individual to individual or from time to time, there can be different quantities of conflict present immediately prior to the decision to act (or not act) aggressively. The effects of differing amounts of conflict may be seen in the length of time it takes the actor to decide which behavior to engage in and in the intensity of the act. It is proposed that the more conflict present in any given situation, the longer it will take to decide whether to act aggressively or not. Although very few studies have measured the time it takes to respond aggressively, it is expected to be longer in high conflict situations than in low. This may be due to the need to consider more elements and to resolve the conflict more fully prior to behaving overtly. In addition, when conflict is high, there will be more postbehavior cognitive consequences of the act. When there are both many and strong reasons to act aggressively combined with many and potent reasons for not acting aggressively, conflict is high and the mental work required to resolve the conflict in the actor's mind is considerable. Once the decision has been made to act aggressively, the intensity of the act will be stronger than if conflict were less. It is proposed that this is because of the need to justify one's actions, and there is less justification for violence in high than in low conflict situations.[30] Thus, high conflict situations lead us to the following hypotheses: (a) the more conflict present in the system, the longer it takes for the individual to act; (b) the more conflict present in the system, the more intense the aggression; (c) the more conflict, the more cognitive consequences of the aggression, such as in re-evaluation of the situation, the action, or the victim. These ideas are explored more fully in Chapters 3 and 4.

We turn now to a detailed examination of each of the four components of the model plus an examination of related phenomena which complement the model.

LONG-TERM FACTORS ASSOCIATED WITH AGGRESSION

2

All of us black people who lived in the neighborhood hated Jews, not because they exploited us, but because we had been taught at home and in Sunday school that Jews were "Christ killers." With the Jews thus singled out for us, we made them fair game for ridicule. We black children—seven, eight, and nine years of age—used to run to the Jew's store and shout:

> *Jew, Jew, Jew*
> *What do you chew?*

. . . And when the baldheaded proprietor would pass by, we black children, poor, half-starved, ignorant, victims of racial prejudice, would sing with a proud lilt:

> *A rotten egg*
> *Never fries*
> *A cheating dog*
> *Never thrives.*

There were many more folk ditties, some mean, others filthy, all of them cruel. No one ever thought of questioning our right to do this; our mothers and parents generally approved, either actively or passively. To hold an attitude of antagonism or distrust toward

Jews was bred in us from childhood; it was not merely racial prej-
udice, it was a part of our cultural heritage.

Richard Wright[1]

Although any person's level of aggression is likely to increase or
decrease depending on the circumstances, some people are more
likely to be aggressive than others; in other words, some people
are more prone to violence or have higher chronic levels of aggressiveness than others. The things that make this so are considered in this chapter. We will examine a number of factors,
most of them influential during childhood, which are positively
related to violence in later life. Among these will be the learning
of aggression and aggression-related norms and attitudes from
parents, peers, and impersonal models. Impersonal models for
learning aggressive norms include violent figures—real or fictitious—portrayed in the mass media as well as those in the society at large, in sports, and in entertainment.

First, it would be prudent to examine the degree to which individuals differ in their levels of violence; how much more violent is one person than any other? The differences between
people's aggressiveness are, in fact, relatively slight and are more
apparent than actual. In the United States, most parents physically punish their children on occasion, and the difference between simple discipline and child abuse is found to be more a
matter of degree than of any qualitative type of behavior. Men
imprisoned for crimes of violence are frequently first offenders,
and it has been argued that the difference between a case of
assault and battery and of homicide is simply the ready availability of a lethal weapon.[2] While there are obvious, and often
highly publicized, cases of individuals with long histories of violence, most acts of violence are committed by relatively average
people with no such past. One explanation of what leads one person and not another to become violent will be seen in Chapter 3
to depend on conditions in the individual's immediate environment. The point I wish to make here is only that the differences
between most people on level of aggression are slight, but that

often slight differences in degree mark the difference between legal, socially acceptable forms of behavior, and criminality.

To summarize, the following points are offered: (a) each person engages in acts which are more or less violent, depending on the circumstances; (b) each person has a characteristic or chronic level of aggressiveness, so that over a long period of time he or she may be more (or less) aggressive than other people. In statistical terms, we can speak of this as an individual's *modal level of aggression;** (c) most people are fairly close to one another in terms of their modal levels of aggression. Differences in the modal level of aggression between people will be discussed in the present chapter, while differences in the aggressiveness level of any given individual at different times will be discussed in Chapter 3.

LEARNING AGGRESSION

As Feshbach[3] has stated: "All theoretical models of aggression assume that aggressive behavior is, to some degree, acquired. The disagreements among theorists lie in the importance ascribed to learning as a determinant of aggression and in the kinds of aggressive behavior that are assumed to be influenced by past learning" (p. 173). In this section, we will examine the means by which aggressive behavior and related norms and attitudes are learned.

A distinction is made by theorists of learning between classical and operant learning or conditioning. In *classical conditioning,* some neutral object is paired with an object which normally causes a particular response. After repeated pairings, the neutral object is then capable of leading to this same response. This type of learning was first described in the classic studies of Pavlov (1849-1936).[4] In Pavlov's experiments, dogs, which normally

---

* The mode is one kind of statistical average. It refers to the most frequent or typical item in a series. The modal level of aggression is the typical level of aggression shown by an individual in a wide variety of situations and under a wide variety of circumstances.

salivate when presented with food, came to salivate at the sound
of a bell after it had been presented several times in conjunction
with the food.

A second kind of learning, most often associated with B. F.
Skinner of Harvard, but which can be traced to the psychologist
E. L. Thorndike (1874-1949), is called *operant conditioning*.
In this type of learning, rewards presented to an actor after a
response is made serve to strengthen that response and increase
the likelihood that it will occur again, while punishments presented after a response decrease the probability that the response
will be repeated. Naturally, there are variations on and complexities to these basic procedures, but these two types of learning
form the basis for most of the behavior patterns that relatively
simple organisms, like animals and infants, acquire. Further, it
has been shown that aggressive behavior patterns learned by
young children are likely to persist into adulthood, particularly
so for males.[5]

Aggressive behavior—and more importantly, norms, values,
beliefs, and attitudes about aggression—can be learned from
one's parents and later from teachers and peers through classical
and operant processes and imitation. If aggression is spoken of
in favorable terms by one's parents, for example, then the concept will come to have positive value for the child.[6] If a child is
encouraged to be or is rewarded for being aggressive, then the
child is likely to increase his or her use of aggressive behavior in
future encounters with others.[7]

In most situations, though, children are not provided with
indiscriminate rewards for acting aggressively nor is aggression
spoken of in the home in uniformly favorable terms. Rather,
parents, teachers, and peers may reward or speak approvingly of
aggression directed toward particular targets, such as some Jews
or blacks, but offer no such rewards or approval for aggression
directed toward other Jews or blacks. There are two consequences of such discriminations. First, the child may perceive
the behaviors of others as inconsistent with regard to when aggression is appropriate, or those who do reward the child may,

in fact, be inconsistent in their actions. Such inconsistency, particularly from parents, is frequently seen as one cause of aggressive behavior among children.[8] Second, the distinctions between targets made by others, while they may to some extent be adopted by the child, are likely to be rather fragile and tenuous, that is, the fine distinctions which adults may make with regard to targets of aggression the child may be cognitively unable to make or maintain. Therefore, "acceptable" aggression directed toward, say, Jews, may generalize to other targets, such as members of other religious minorities. However, the learned targets of aggression defined as acceptable will more often serve as victims than other targets to which the learning generalizes.

In the same way that children learn which groups or individuals are considered appropriate targets of aggression by their parents and peers, they also learn to value (or devalue) weapons and other means of aggressing, the circumstances under which aggression is considered appropriate, and attitudes toward the police and the law.[9]

A well-known study by Sears, Maccoby, and Levin[10] examined child-rearing practices and children's aggressive behavior. Nearly four hundred mothers of kindergarten children were interviewed about their use of disciplinary measures, their permissiveness toward their children's aggressive, feeding and sexual behavior, and their children's expression of aggression toward peers, siblings, and parents. Among the major findings of the study was that the use of physical punishment by parents was positively related to the amount of aggression shown by the children. When coupled with high permissiveness toward the children's behavior, high punishment was even more strongly associated with children's aggression. Over one-third of the girls and two-fifths of the boys rated as highly aggressive came from homes in which parents relied on physical punishment as a disciplinary measure and also were highly permissive.

Although the methodology of this study may have some shortcomings,[11] it raises questions about the use of physical punishment in child-rearing. According to traditional learning theory, if children are punished for being aggressive, they should then refrain from aggressing in the future. Yes, the results of research on punishment and children's aggression often find that punishment only begets aggression. What, if anything, do children learn when they are punished for some transgression? In order to answer this question, we will have to examine what has come to be known as social learning theory as developed by Albert Bandura of Stanford University.

SOCIAL LEARNING THEORY

According to Bandura,[12] children learn not only from direct rewards and punishments, but also from observation. It would take children considerably longer to learn to speak if they had to rely solely on rewards and punishments for correct and incorrect verbal utterances; instead, they are able to imitate the verbal speech patterns of those around them. The ability to imitate is seen as one mechanism by which learning can occur. As Bandura states, "it is difficult to imagine a socialization process in which the language, mores, vocational activities, familial customs, and the educational, religious, and political practices of a culture are taught to each new member by selective reinforcement of fortuitous behaviors, without benefit of models who exemplify the cultural patterns in their own behavior" (p. 5).

Models, that is, others whose behavior serves as a guide to observers, are capable of teaching both concrete actions as well as abstract concepts to a child. Obviously, the most important models are a child's parents, from whom the child acquires a wide variety of behavior patterns, attitudes, values, and norms. According to substantial research by Bandura and others,[13] a child will learn behavior which it observes in others, providing that neither the others nor the child-observer are punished for that behavior.

In the case of a parent spanking a child for behaving aggressively, a conflict is actually presented to the child. On the one hand, the child is "told," via the punishment, that aggression is bad. On the other hand, the child observes the parent acting aggressively. In such a case, the child is likely to learn not to suppress his aggression but to use aggression to influence the behavior of others. Children are more likely to do what their parents do than what their parents say they should do. Naturally, if a child is punished by its parents each time it is caught behaving aggressively, it is likely to learn not to be aggressive in the presence of the parents. The child will also learn that, if its parents use aggression, then at least in some circumstances, aggression is a desirable and appropriate behavior in which to engage. It is not surprising, then, that aggressive parents have aggressive offspring.[14]

However, parents are not the only models in a child's life. If they were, children would be duplicates of their parents, and, as the widely discussed "generation gap" attests, children are often quite different from their parents. The question arises, then, as to what other forces influence the social and moral development of the child. One such force is the behavioral and moral code depicted by others in society at large. Such general social norms are portrayed in the behavior of those real and fictitious people with whom the child comes into contact in real life, in stories, in books, and in television.

Aside from direct reinforcement from and modeling by parents, there seem to be several ways in which social behavior is transmitted to the child. First, and probably most important, is the behavior of adults displayed on television and in the movies. Most children watch at least two hours of television each day.[15] This amounts to a total of over ten months of TV viewing by the time a child is twelve. By the time a child is sixteen, he or she will have spent more time in front of a television set than in school. Advertisers spend hundreds of millions of dollars each year in the belief that television has an effect on people's attitudes and behavior, and it is reasonable to ascertain the effects of such a pervasive medium on the social development of its most ardent viewers, the young. Second, children can learn behavioral and normative patterns from the games and sports which society condones. At home and in school children are encouraged to participate in play activities which may provide general rules of conduct which the children then use in other, nonplay, situations. Other forms of entertainment can also provide the child with rules of conduct. The behavior of people whom the child sees or hears about provide the child with expectations and norms which guide his or her actions. Each of these forms and means of social learning will be reviewed below.

Might Makes Right: Teaching Violence by Mass Media

More research has been conducted on the effects of violence in the mass media than on almost any other topic in the realm of human aggression. Despite nearly two decades of research, controversy and debate still rage over the effects of portrayed violence on aggressive behavior. Part of the debate involves purely philosophical arguments, while a portion of it revolves around the research methodology involved. In general, however, the research is quite consistent and does warrant some firm conclusions about the effects of mass media on human aggression. First, it will be necessary to examine the philosophical issues about which so much misunderstanding has arisen.

Science is not a proscriptive enterprise but a descriptive one; it can describe reality and in many instances predict future realities, but it cannot say in any manner what reality ought to be like. Furthermore, from the time of the philosopher David Hume (1711-1776), who pointed out that "knowledge" of the future must be of a different sort than knowledge of the past, scientists have tended to couch statements about future events in terms of probabilities rather than certainties. Therefore, with regard to the effects of mass media violence, it would be possible to demonstrate that media violence has caused people to act aggressively in the past, but it would not be possible to assert with certainty that it will cause people to act aggressively in the future. The best that any science can do is say that there is a certain probability that it will do so. In addition, it is not possible for science to make value judgments about whether violence ought or ought not to be presented in the mass media. Clearly, for such proscriptions, other than scientific criteria must be invoked. (See Chapter 5.)

The other issue which beclouds discussions of media violence involves the nature of various types of research. Essentially, psychological research can be divided into two types, correlational and experimental. In experimental research, the researcher is able to manipulate one or more variables by exposing some research subjects to some stimuli and by exposing other subjects to different stimuli. In this way, one can more readily determine the effects of such stimuli on behavior. In correlational research, the researcher does not have the freedom to control which of his subjects is exposed to what stimuli, and because he lacks such control, the issue of causality becomes much more ambiguous. In an experimental study on the effects of media violence, research subjects might be divided into two groups, with one of them exposed to violent media episodes and the other exposed to nonviolent media episodes. If the first group behaves more aggressively than the second following media exposure, it can be argued that, other things being equal between the two groups, the media violence was the cause of the aggression. In a correlational study, where it is not possible to control what media episodes subjects are exposed to, the researcher is likely to measure the extent to which people voluntarily view media violence and the extent to which they are aggressive. He can then correlate these two variables in order to determine whether those who are aggressive tend to view more media violence than those who are not aggressive.* The difficulties with such a correlational study are (a) that it is a possibility, not that media violence causes aggres-

---

* A correlation is a statistic indicating the degree of relationship between two (or more) different variables. A correlation can range anywhere from minus one to plus one. The more divergent the correlation coefficient is from zero, the stronger the relationship between variables. A positive correlation indicates that the relationship between variables is direct (that is, as one variable increases the other increases), whereas a negative correlation indicates that the relationship is inverse (as one variable increases, the other decreases).

sion but that aggressive people tend to watch aggressive media
episodes and (b) that both the tendency to behave aggressively
and the tendency to watch media violence are caused by some
third variable such as boredom or neglectful parents.

The Surgeon General's Advisory Committee on Television
and Social Behavior[16] was well aware of these scientific limita-
tions and therefore was quite cautious—some have argued overly
cautious—in stating that television violence causes aggression
among observers. The problem is that it is impossible scientifically to *prove* that TV violence causes aggression. What we can
state within the limits of science is that there is a high probability that TV violence causes aggression.

What is the evidence with respect to media violence? Liebert[17]
has summarized the pertinent research:

> The data suggest consistently that children are exposed to a
> heavy dose of violence on television. It is also clear that they
> can and do-retain some of the aggressive behaviors which they
> see, and are often able to reproduce them. Differences in recall
> as a function of age are in the expected direction (better recall
> with increasing age). Differences in recall as a function of con-
> tent are less clearly understood, but violent content appears to
> be learned and remembered at least as well as nonviolent fare.
> . . . Punishment to an aggressive model leads children to
> avoid reproduction of the exemplary behavior, but does not
> prevent learning or subsequent performance under more favor-
> able circumstances. . . . It is important to note that the corre-
> lational results, while generally consistent, point to a moderate
> (rather than a strong) relationship between watching tele-
> vision violence and subsequent aggressive attitudes and be-
> havior (pp. 27-28).[18]

In order to provide the reader with a deeper appreciation of
the research in the area of media violence, one of the studies
which has had a major impact on subsequent research and
theory will be reviewed in detail. In a study by Albert Bandura,
published in 1965,[19] sixty-six nursery school children were ex-

posed to one of three five-minute films on a TV console. In all three films an adult enacted a series of verbal and physical attacks on a plastic Bobo doll (a large inflatable doll with a painted face and a sand base). One group of children observed the model rewarded following the aggression with candy and soft drinks. A second group of children saw the model punished following the aggression with spanking and verbal rebukes. A third group of children saw only the model's aggressive behavior with no rewarding or punishing consequences. The children were then allowed to play for ten minutes in a room which contained, among other toys, a Bobo doll. During the play period, the children's aggressive behaviors were observed and recorded. Following the free-play period, children were told that they would receive fruit juices and picture booklets if they would imitate the behavior that they had seen in the film. The children's aggression during the free-play period is an index of the extent to which the films influenced "spontaneous" aggression, while their behavior during the last phase of the study represents the extent to which they learned and could reproduce the aggressive behavior they had seen in the films. Spontaneous aggression was greatest in the groups which had seen the model rewarded and which had seen the aggression without any reinforcing consequences; it was least in the group which had seen the model punished for aggression. Thus, punishment may serve to inhibit spontaneous aggression among children-observers. When asked to imitate the aggression they had seen, all three groups of children were equally able to duplicate the model's aggressive performance. Thus, learning of aggression took place regardless of whether the model was rewarded, punished, or neither.

The implications of this study are many and varied. They indicate that children are capable of learning what they see, regardless of the presence of rewards or punishments. Second, the results suggest that children are likely to imitate the aggressive behavior they observe in mass media providing that the aggressor was not punished for his or her actions. Finally, the results indicate that, contrary to many theories of learning, new forms of behavior can be acquired in the absence of rewards.

A considerable number of studies have been conducted along the lines of the Bandura experiment, most of which were designed to determine whether observers, either children or adults, could (or would) imitate the aggressive behavior depicted in mass media. With only occasional exceptions[20] such studies have demonstrated that media violence is capable of producing real-life violence.

The evidence for a reduction or catharsis of aggression following observation of violence is far outweighed by the scores of studies reporting that the observation of violence serves to stimulate aggression. It is conceivable, however, that a kind of catharsis does occur under some, as yet unspecified, conditions. For example, immediately after I had first seen the film *Bonnie and Clyde* there was little question in my mind that I was, at that moment, less likely to be aggressive than immediately prior to seeing the film. I felt emotionally numb after the final scene in which Bonnie and Clyde were gunned down. In fact, it took a few minutes before I felt able to leave the theater and begin the drive home. In thinking over my reactions to the film, I began to question whether what I had experienced was a catharsis of aggression. Had someone been conducting a study at that movie, he would probably have found that viewers were less violent immediately after having seen the film. However, I suspect that had our mythical researcher measured responses other than aggression, such as altruism or hunger or practically anything else, he would also have found a depressant effect of the film. Instead of a catharsis of aggression, I think the film produced a dulling of emotions in general. In order for a genuine aggression catharsis to occur, there should be a reduction in aggressiveness but not in other, unrelated responses. What had first appeared to me to be an aggression catharsis in retrospect seems to have been an overall reduction in general emotional activation. For this reason, research on aggression should measure at least one nonaggressive response in order to determine whether the effects observed are specific to aggressive behavior or not.

In addition, many of the laboratory experiments on imitation of media violence have been criticized on methodological grounds, largely because the research laboratory is an artificial environment and because most laboratory experiments use excerpts of violent scenes taken out of context from the film or TV program.[21] Finally, nearly every study on effects of media violence has been conducted using only Americans as research subjects, and there is the question of the generality and pervasiveness of the results.

Together with my colleagues Ralph Rosnow and Tamas Raday of Temple University, Irwin Silverman of York University, Toronto, and George Gaskell of the London School of Economics, I conducted a media-aggression study in four countries (Canada, England, Italy, and the United States), using a natural, nonlaboratory research setting, with full-length films.[22] We chose films playing in each country which were aggressive (such as *Clockwork Orange* and *Straw Dogs*), or which were equally arousing, but nonaggressive (such as *The Decameron*), or which were neither arousing nor aggressive (such as *Fiddler on the Roof* and *Living Free*). We interviewed adult males either before or after they had seen one of these films. The interview was designed to assess the viewer's level of punitiveness, which was used as an index of aggressiveness. For example, we asked our subjects to assign minimum prison sentences for persons convicted of various crimes, and more severe prison sentences were taken to imply more punitiveness on the part of subjects. The results indicated that there was a statistically significant increase in this aggressiveness measure after viewing an aggressive film in all four countries, while there was a general decrease in aggressiveness after viewing a nonarousing, nonaggressive film. Sexual films had no appreciable effect on observers' levels of punitiveness (see Figure 2.1). The study as a whole indicates that (a) aggressive films have an effect on viewers' levels of aggression; (b) the results are not peculiar to Americans, but

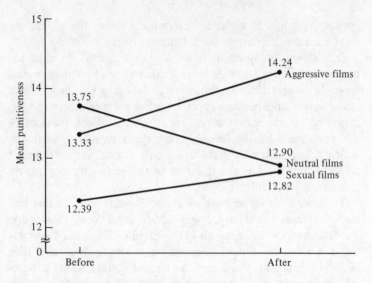

Figure 2.1. Effects of film content on aggression. Data adapted from Goldstein, Rosnow, Raday, Silverman, and Gaskell. By permission of Mouton Publishers, The Hague, Paris.

also hold for Canadian, English, and Italian viewers; (c) the increase in aggressiveness was due to the aggressive content of the film rather than to its arousing qualities, since arousing but nonaggressive (that is, sexual) films did not influence observers' aggressiveness levels. As an additional part of the study, some of the nearly 900 subjects in this experiment were asked to donate money to charity either before or after watching one of the films. There were no significant changes in charitableness as a result of any of the films. This is evidence for the fact that the aggressive films may have an influence only on subjects' levels of aggressiveness, rather than have a general effect on all behaviors.

The research having demonstrated that media violence can influence aggressive behavior, a number of additional questions become prominent. For example, does media violence influence some people more than others? Why is there so much violence on television and in movies and in books? What other behaviors and attitudes are influenced by modeling and imitation?

Television viewing does not occur in a vacuum but rather takes place within a family context. The importance, meaning, and psychological experience of watching television will depend upon the quality of one's home environment, just as the nature of so many other behaviors are influenced by family interactions.

Largely because of learning unrelated to TV viewing, males seem to respond to TV violence to a greater degree than females. In the Bandura study summarized earlier, both spontaneous and learned aggression were found to be greatest for boys. This is probably because boys are provided with greater rewards for aggression than girls and because boys are more apt to identify with adult males and thus have more numerous aggressive models to emulate than girls. The quality of parental training also influences the effects of televised violence. Chaffee and McLeod[23] report that in families where nonaggression is stressed (for example, where parents teach their children not to be mean to others), there is only a slight relationship between viewing media violence and aggressive behavior in children (although the relationship is still a positive one). In families where there is no stress placed on nonaggression, there is a strong relationship between viewing TV violence and aggressive behavior. Another way of stating this is that in homes where parents serve as strong nonaggressive models for their children, televised models will be relatively uninfluential; where parents do not serve as nonaggressive models or where parents encourage aggression, televised models will either take precedence over parental models or will serve to further strengthen the child's aggression. If mass media models contradict parental models, it is likely that the parental models will be more influential, since it is the parents who directly control the child's rewards and punishments. It has often been suggested that the influence of mass media violence is greatest for young children who are unable to distinguish reality from fantasy. The research on this question, however, fails to support this contention. Even while recognizing that violence on television is fictional and staged, adults too have been found to become more aggressive following exposure to media violence.[24]

It has also been argued that whatever influence televised violence has, it is short-lived. Again, the research indicates that, to the contrary, the effects of exposure to media violence may persist for at least four to five months.[25]

Attraction to Violence, or,
What's Playing at Your Neighborhood Drive-In?

If media violence is so likely to have detrimental effects on social behavior, why is it so prevalent and why do people expose themselves to it with such regularity? It is a very curious phenomenon that people who, for the most part, consider themselves peaceable feed on violence so often and in so many forms. As the Hearst newspapers discovered long ago, spectacular and violent headlines sell papers, and as the entertainment industries discovered more recently, violence in movies, television programming, comic books, and novels produces sizeable profits. Clark and Blankenburg[26] found a strong and positive relationship between the per cent of TV programs classified as violent in any given year and the average Nielsen ratings for that year. In addition to the fictional portrayal of violence, people are attracted to more direct forms of aggression. Children play with toy weapons, adults rush to the scene of a conflagration and gather in large numbers to watch a threatened suicide or the aftermath of a violent crime. Nearly thirty million people attended professional football games in 1972, and probably three times that number watched them on television. Boxing matches, particularly those involving heavyweights, are broadcast by satellite to millions of people, and soccer is the world's number one spectator sport. It is undeniable that a good many people find violence appealing rather than appalling.

About a year ago, the Philadelphia newspapers carried an advertisement for a forthcoming movie, *The Mark of the Devil,* which was described as "Positively the most horrifying film ever made. The first film rated V for violence." The ad is reproduced in Figure 2.2. As I happened to be in the neighborhood when the film opened, I was curious to see who would attend *The Mark of the Devil.* I was surprised to see a very long line before the box office. Most of those in line were boys in their early teens, and nearly all of them were black.

Although Philadelphia has a fairly large middle-class black population, it seems reasonable to argue that most blacks in the city live in less than safe, middle-class neighborhoods. Why should young blacks, who are undoubtedly exposed to considerable violence in their schools and neighborhoods, pay to see a film advertised as extraordinarily violent? I could think of only a few possible explanations: If we assume, as many do, that there is an innate aggressive drive which must find expression, then violent events may serve as safety valves which indirectly discharge aggressive impulses in ways which are not socially disruptive. We have seen in Chapter 1, however, that it is quite unlikely that such an explanation is valid; the evidence largely disputes the notion of an aggression instinct. Another explanation for the attraction to violence is based on increased familiarity with real violence in daily life.[27] It may be that art imitates life, in the same way that research on mass media violence, such as the studies by Bandura, suggest that life imitates art. It seemed reasonable that familiarity with violence simply had the effect of making violence salient, meaningful, and attractive. A third reason for the appeal of media violence is that it provides excitement and arousal which may be missing from one's daily routine. Furthermore, perhaps witnessing fictional violence can help a person cope with the real violence to which he is exposed; one might learn from the film's characters that violence can be overcome, that it is not really to be feared.

Intrigued by these possibilities, I reviewed the research literature to determine whether there had been any research on attraction to violence. Only one study could be found. Following the

POSITIVELY THE MOST HORRIFYING FILM EVER MADE

Guaranteed to upset your stomach

mark of the devil

the first film rated V* for violence

DUE TO THE HORRIFYING SCENES NO ONE ADMITTED WITHOUT A VOMIT BAG

(available free at box office)

* ALL AGES ADMITTED / PARENTAL ESCORTS ENCOURAGED

DISTRIBUTED BY: HALLMARK RELEASING CORP.

murder of a coed on the University of Wisconsin campus, three social psychologists conducted a study on movie preference.[28] There were two films playing locally during the week of the murder, one a violent film (*In Cold Blood*) and one based on a D. H. Lawrence story (*The Fox*). The researchers report an increase in attendance at the violent film among coeds following the murder, but no such increase at the nonviolent film. They explain these results by suggesting that the film would help the girls to cope with their fear by exposing them to violence which would be harmless to them personally. As the authors themselves mention, however, there are a number of other possible explanations for these results, and so I decided to conduct another study which examined preference for aggressive films.[29]

In this study, college students read one of three prose passages—aggressive, sexual, or neutral (that is, neither aggressive nor sexual). They were then asked to indicate which movies from a list of three aggressive, three sexual, and three neutral movies they would most like to see. The results indicated that subjects who read the aggressive passage preferred aggressive movies to all others. Those subjects who read the sexual passage showed the greatest desire to see sexual films, and those who read the neutral passage least preferred to see sexual and aggressive films. It would seem that prior experience with aggression is positively related to a preference for aggressive movie content.

There thus seems to be a continuous interplay between media violence and real violence, with an exposure to either one contributing in some measure to the other. For at least some people, exposure to media violence contributes to aggressive behavior; and for people exposed to some episodes of real violence, there is an increased preference for violent portrayals in the mass media.

Figure 2.2. Advertisement for *Mark of the Devil*. Reprinted by permission of Hallmark Pictures, Boston, Massachusetts.

The Role of Modeling and Imitation in
Impulsivity and Self-Control of Aggression

One important abstract behavior style related to aggression is an individual's impulsiveness. As Mischel[30] states, "Even the simplest, most primitive steps in socialization require learning to defer one's impulses and to express them only under special conditions of time and place, as seen in toilet training. Similarly, enormously complex chains of deferred gratification are required for people to achieve the delayed rewards provided by our culture's social system and institutions" (p. 380).

The inability to delay gratification—impulsivity—is both directly and indirectly related to aggression and criminality.[31] As Mischel notes, many rewards provided by society require the ability to postpone immediate but small rewards for long-term but larger rewards. For example, high paying jobs require planning, extended education, training, and apprenticeship. The inability to make such long-range plans and immediate sacrifices would all but preclude an individual's attainment of high occupational status. Those who lack the ability to plan for the future may be deprived of the means by which to obtain desirable social goals. Thus deprived of socially acceptable means, highly impulsive people may "improvise" their own means to such desirable goals as money, status, and power. This analysis is similar to and complements one proposed by Robert K. Merton[32] a sociologist at Columbia University. Merton discusses, under the heading of "innovation," those in society who desire socially defined goals, such as wealth, but who lack socially approved means of attaining those goals. In this situation, individuals will provide innovative means for achieving goals which may be socially deviant or criminal.

In addition to instituting their own socially deviant means to social goals, highly impulsive people are also likely to react with aggression to interpersonal difficulties. Violence is a tempting and impulsive solution to interpersonal problems. It is tempting because it has the effect of reducing the complexities and subtleties normally found in human problems to a simple contest of strength and agility. In reducing complex interpersonal confrontations to simple physical contests, their multifaceted nature need not be considered. Reason and restraint in the face of difficulties indicate that one recognizes more than one side to a problem and that compromise might be a reasonable way to settle the dispute. Communication and compromise between disputants is often a tedious, long, and complex process, particularly so if the parties begin from different vantage points. Differences of opinion, if not of fact, make one's arguments likely to distortion and misinterpretation by those who hold divergent views.

How can delay of gratification or impulsivity be learned? An important experiment by Bandura and Mischel[33] demonstrates that it can be acquired through processes of imitation and modeling. Children with little tendency to delay gratification were exposed to a model who, when given a choice between an immediate small reward and a future larger reward, chose the latter. Children who tended to delay gratification were exposed to a model who chose the immediate small reward. Both groups of children, when tested following exposure to the respective models, showed significant changes. Low delay of gratification observers became better able to delay immediate gratification, while children initially high in delay of gratification tended to become lower. These results suggest that the kinds of postponement and planning for rewards demonstrated by parents and others to whom the child is exposed will influence the child's own such tendencies.

As with the effects of aggressive models, the family's social environment mediates the child's responses to delay of gratification in models. In particular, the child's expectations of and trust in others influences his impulsivity. To the extent that the child has trust in others, there is a tendency to imitate modeled delay of gratification; when trust in others is absent, the child will tend to be impulsive and low in the ability to postpone immediate rewards.[34]

Impulsive behavior implies that conscious, cognitive mechanisms which normally influence behavior are absent. What psychologists refer to as cognitive control over behavior, and what we generally call self-control, is minimized when a person acts impulsively. Rather than taking the time to decide among several possible alternatives and rather than trying to imagine the consequences of one's actions for oneself and the others involved, impulsive behavior is spontaneous, with little or no cognitive forethought involved. Self- or cognitive-control over behavior is what marks man as a rational being; the inability to foresee the consequences and the context of one's behavior reduce man's rationality. Impulsive behavior diminishes rationality, and anything which reduces self-control over behavior increases impulsivity.

Aggression in Sports

Games and sports serve a variety of functions—from teaching young participants to abide by formally proscribed rules of conduct to the fostering of competition between teams and cooperation within teams. Both participants and spectators may learn abstract principles for behavior from the rules of games. When discussing aggression in sports, it is well to keep in mind that sports have many levels, only one of which may be aggressive. Indeed, aggression of any sort may be totally absent from a great many sports and games. With respect to those sports which require bodily contact between participants of opposing teams, it is possible that for some (or even all) players and for some spectators (but certainly not all), the aggression inherent in contact sports is peripheral to other facets of the game. It is reasonable that for some players and perhaps for some spectators, the violence of, say, a football game, can be transcended through involvement in the game and in this way have little effect on the spectators' or players' levels of aggression. For a great many spectators and players, however, aggression in contact sports does have an effect.

There have been numerous occasions when violence has

erupted at athletic events. Lever[35] has suggested that the war between El Salvador and Honduras may be traced to a soccer match between those countries. In 1964, a riot erupted at a soccer match in Lima, Peru, in which 300 people were killed. Riots have broken out at boxing matches in New York and Philadelphia. In 1970 in Ottawa and in 1972 in Philadelphia hockey fans rioted after opposing players became involved in a fight. Because of the frequency with which fights had erupted at high school basketball games, Dayton, Ohio, games were played behind closed doors with no spectators allowed. It is not difficult to find comparable occurrences, at boxing and soccer matches and hockey and football games throughout the world. At the same time, it is quite rare to find such violence taking place at tennis, gymnastics, or horse racing events. One quite obvious difference between these two groups of sports—those at which violence erupts and those at which it is rare—is that the former tend to be the more violent sports.

Crook[36] has noted that

the behavior of crowds watching "conventionally" competitive sports often indicates the arousal of aggressive attitudes rather than their happy sublimation. . . . The wanton destruction of train interiors by British football team supporters . . . reveals a release of social tensions in what would appear to be highly convivial surroundings. Indeed, the holding of major sporting events is often manageable only when effective rules of crowd control are operative (pp. 173-74).

We can consider whether the physical contact of boxing, football, hockey, and soccer in any way causes these violent outbursts. And we can also consider a larger issue involved in aggressive sports, that is, the extent to which they provide social support for aggression in general. Thus, we can inquire into both the immediate, short-term effects as well as the general, long-term effects of aggression in sports.

As we have seen in the studies on mass media violence, observers tend to learn and imitate the violence they witness on the movie and television screens, and it would be reasonable to expect that watching violence in sports, like watching it on TV, tends to increase the likelihood of observers' becoming aggressive. Further, we have seen that the effects of televised violence are not necessarily immediate, but may develop later and persist for quite some time. There is no sound reason for suspecting that the effects of violence in sports differ from the effects of violence in other forms of entertainment.

However, a number of students of human behavior have suggested, to the contrary, that participation in and observation of aggressive sports serve as safety valves which tend to reduce participants' and observers' levels of aggression. Among those who have proposed that catharsis of aggression occurs have been William James, Freud, Ardrey, and Lorenz.[37] Storr[38] has proposed that "rivalry between nations in sports can do nothing but good" (pp. 132-33). Of course, if these theories are incorrect and observing or acting out violence causes an increase, rather than a decrease, in aggressiveness, then their suggested policies of fostering international competition are not only incorrect, but potentially disastrous; while trying to reduce aggressiveness, they will actually increase it.

There are, besides these two extreme positions (the one suggesting that watching aggressive sports uniformly leads to an increase in aggression, and the other suggesting that it leads to a reduction), several intermediate theoretical positions. Based on the frustration-aggression theory of Dollard and his colleagues at Yale, it would be expected that watching aggression would lead to an increase in aggression only for those observers who are in some way frustrated. At a soccer match or football game, for example, it would be frustrating if a person wanted Team A to win while Team B actually won. Thus, we might predict that only those spectators whose preferred team loses a game would show an increase in aggression, while those whose preferred team wins would show no increase, or perhaps even a decrease, in aggression.

Following the study of Bandura elaborated earlier, we might consider that watching a team lose a game in an aggressive sport is in some way perceived as a "punishment" for their behavior, while watching a team win a game is perceived as a "reward" for their behavior. If this can be applied to an aggressive sport, we might expect that those who watch their preferred team win a game will actually become more aggressive than those who watch their preferred team lose the game since those in favor of the winning side have seen their players (models) rewarded for their aggression, while those favoring the losing side have seen their team punished for its aggression.

In order to examine these various possibilities, Robert Arms and I conducted a study at the 1969 Army-Navy football game, in which we measured male spectators' levels of hostility before and after the game.[39] As a control group we also measured hostility among spectators before or after they had observed an Army-Temple gymnastics competition. This nonaggressive sport served as a check on the possibility that watching *any* sport for two or three hours would lead to an increase in aggressiveness. We obtained hostility scores from 150 spectators at the football game, 97 of them before the game and 53 following the game. We also obtained information about their favored team and their level of involvement in the game. At the gymnastics meet we obtained comparable kinds of information from 81 male spectators, 49 before and 32 after viewing the meet. The major findings of the study, shown in Table 2-1, indicate a significant increase in hostility for spectators at the football game and no such increase for those observing a gym meet. The increase in hostility at the football game did not depend upon whether the spectators' preferred team won or lost or on whether they even cared who won or lost; all groups of spectators interviewed after the game had a higher hostility score than those interviewed before. It will be noted that the increase for the pro-Army subjects was greater than that for the pro-Navy subjects. The largest increase in hostility, then, was for those who favored the winning

TABLE 2.1

Hostility at aggressive and nonaggressive sports

| | Football game Preferred team | | | |
	Army (winning team)	Navy (losing team)	No preference	Gym meet
Pre-game	10.42	11.72	11.67	12.00
Post-game	13.33	13.17	15.00	12.71

Note: The higher the score, the more hostile the subjects. Each entry is the mean hostility for subjects in that group. Adapted from Goldstein & Arms.

team rather than the losing team. This finding lends support to the social learning and imitation theory of Bandura. The pro-Army fans saw Army players rewarded for their aggression on the field, while pro-Navy fans saw their team punished (by being beaten) for their aggression. Thus, the vicarious reward served to heighten Army fans' aggressiveness and the vicarious punishment served to inhibit to some degree the aggressiveness of Navy fans (although the latter still showed a significant increase in hostility).

The following conclusions seem warranted by the data of the Army-Navy study. First, that the vicarious catharsis predicted by James, Freud, Ardrey, Lorenz, Storr, and others, has not been found to occur. Of course, there may be some people who do show such an effect, and since we obtained data from each subject only once in the study (either before or after the game) we have no way of determining whether this occurred. On the whole, however, there was no evidence of a catharsis effect. Second, since all groups of spectators at the football game showed an increase in hostility, it does not seem likely that frustration or anger is a necessary condition for this effect to occur. On the contrary, the nonfrustrated spectators showed almost twice the increase in hostility as the frustrated spectators. This finding is consistent with Bandura's discussion of vicarious reinforcement. But further research is needed on this point before any definitive statement can be made about the reinforcing effects of observing wins and losses in sports.[40]

A question I have often been asked since the Army-Navy study was published is what the findings mean in practical terms. Although we will consider some of the implications of the study in Chapter 6, it can be stated here that the results do not mean that anyone who watches an aggressive sport will go home and beat his wife. The measure of hostility used in the study was a verbal one, obtained by means of a brief questionnaire, and is only an index of overt aggression. The results do mean that one is *more likely* to be aggressive after having seen a violent sport. In this way, a violent sport serves more as a situational influence on an individual's aggression than as a long-term influence. A person who watches a violent sport may be more predisposed to violence afterward, but this tendency is more likely to last for only minutes or hours than for weeks or months. On the other hand, if we consider repeated exposure to violent sports there may well be a long-term effect on a person's chronic level of aggression. As Merton[41] has written, "In competitive athletics, when the aim of victory is shorn of its institutional trappings and success becomes construed as 'winning the game' rather than 'winning under the rules of the game,' a premium is implicitly set upon the use of illegitimate but technically efficient means." To the degree that aggression in sports is excessive, observers are likely to learn that it is to some extent acceptable and legitimate as a means of winning whatever game the spectator happens to play. This is particularly true in professional sports where players are highly paid and often the amount of their salary is commensurate with the amount of aggression displayed on the playing field. The advertisement for the Philadelphia Blazers hockey club shown in Figure 2.3 can only serve to legitimize aggression as a means to the desirable goal of winning.

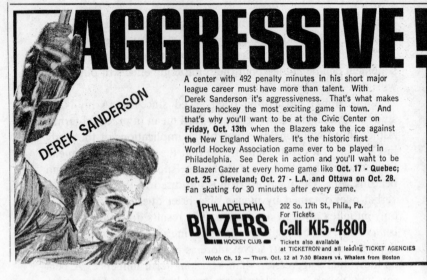

Figure 2.3. Advertisement for Philadelphia Blazers.

"A MINISTER, A PRIEST, AND A RABBI WERE PLAYING GOLF . . ." : THE CASE OF HOSTILE HUMOR

To what extent is the telling of or laughing at hostile jokes related to other aspects of aggression? At least two questions about aggression and humor seem pertinent to our interests. First, does telling or laughing at an aggressive joke make the teller or recipient more or less aggressive? Second, what psychological meaning can be attributed to telling or laughing at aggressive humor? This usually comes down to the question of whether a person who laughs vociferously at, or who continually tells, aggressive jokes is more aggressive than others who rarely tell or laugh at such humor. The problem of how humor as a whole operates, that is, the dynamics by which a person finds an aggressive joke funny, will not be dealt with at any length here.[42] We will restrict our discussion to aggression and humor.

Effects of Hostile Humor on Aggression

There are a few experiments in the research literature which directly undertake to determine the effects of aggressive humor on the recipient's level of aggressiveness. The initial interest in such studies was the fairly popular conception that aggressive humor serves as one of the "safety valves" of aggression; that by laughing at aggressive humor a person could somehow "let off steam." This effect, known as a catharsis of aggression through humor, has been proposed by Freud, Grotjahn, and Mendel,[43] among others. The underlying argument is that some of the energy which might otherwise be expressed in overt aggression is syphoned off during laughter and thereby serves as a drain on aggressive energy. The net result was theorized to be an overall reduction in potential aggression. Experiments on this humor-catharsis effect have provided almost no support for its occurrence. The best study in this area, by Leonard Berkowitz[44] of the University of Wisconsin, reports that subjects who heard an aggressive Don Rickles tape became more aggressive than those who heard a nonaggressive George Carlin tape. Comparable results have been reported by others using various kinds of humor, including animated cartoon films.[45] These experiments demonstrate that, rather than serving as a drain, aggressive humor actually serves to stimulate aggression. Indeed, it would be surprising if exposure to aggressive humor had different effects than exposure to aggressive sports, television programs, or parents. There is no reason to expect aggressive humor to differ in any qualitative way from other types of aggressive material.[46]

Can some types of humor be used in an aggressive way? Can people use humor as a weapon against others? The answers to these questions deal with a quite different area of humor than the one we have just discussed. We have considered the recipient of an aggressive joke, but what of the joke-teller? It certainly makes sense that people will use aggressive humor as a means of attack against others, particularly those of higher status or with more power than the joke-teller. Here we come up against a major assumption of much humor research. Freud proposed that the effects or functions of a joke were precisely the same for the joke-teller as for the listener. But this assumption has not been tested directly, and may be unwarranted. In fact, the issue of the functions and effects of aggressive humor for the teller and the listener points out that aggressive humor may have different effects on these people. For the recipient of aggressive humor, aggressiveness is significantly increased. However, for the initiator of aggressive humor, different effects may obtain.

We can ask first why someone would tell an aggressive joke. If it is just to amuse others, is passed on from a secondary source, or is elicited by an audience, it is unlikely to have any hostile intent, and it is therefore not aggressive in strict accordance with our definition of aggression. However, when the intention of the joke-teller is hostile, when his or her aim is to psychologically injure or embarrass someone, then the joke will serve precisely the same function as a more direct, physical form of aggression.

Related to the question of why someone might tell an aggressive joke is the issue of whom it might be directed toward. Although research in this area is scanty,[47] it seems that aggressive humor will be directed toward others of higher social position or greater power, such as one's boss or teachers. Gunnar Myrdal[48] notes that much Negro humor in the America of the 1930's and '40's was directed at whites, and Obrdlik[49] notes that many of the jokes circulating among the Czechs in the late 1930's and early '40's were directed against their Nazi oppressors. Theodor Reik[50] argues that the use of aggressive humor by Jews was a most effective weapon against their oppressors and was, in many instances, the only avenue of attack open to them. There is probably good reason for the use of this fairly subtle and indirect form of aggression: it is much less likely to bring about retaliation. Aggression through humor is indirect; if disguised sufficiently it may not even be perceived as hostile by the recipient. And if the recipient should smile or laugh, even though he or she is the butt of the joke, retaliation seems all but precluded.

Still, the question persists as to whether humor with aggressive intent can serve as a cathartic, whether it can actually reduce the "inner level" of aggression felt by the jokester. Since there is no direct measure of residual aggression, it is difficult to determine scientifically if this is the case. I have argued that aggressive humor can be used as a hostile weapon, particularly in situations where more direct aggression would bring retaliation. Whether this only heightens the individual's feelings of anger or whether it serves to reduce them remains unclear. If it is true that telling an aggressive joke, as with listening to one, increases the jokester's level of aggression, then the following should occur: (a) after telling a single hostile joke other hostile jokes will follow and (b) each subsequent hostile joke will be told with increased rapidity, that is, the amount of time elapsed between successive hostile jokes will decrease. Although such a test has not been conducted, a study reported in Chapter 3 by Goldstein, Davis, and Herman,[51] indicates that aggression will lead to more intense aggression on subsequent acts. If aggressive humor is merely one form of aggression, then we ought to expect the same results whether the actor is telling hostile jokes, delivering verbal insults, or shocking another person.

Why Is Aggressive Humor Funny?

It is probably safe to say that most "one-liners" told by monologists and stand-up comics are aggressive in content. Henny Youngman's most famous one-liner, "Now take my wife. Please!" is obviously aggressive in content, if not in intent (he probably doesn't mean it). Don Rickles has built his entire repertoire around the insult, embarrassment, and antagonism of others. Jack E. Leonard, Rickles' comedic forefather, was probably the first modern comic to become famous with insult-as-humor.* Aggressive humor seems to be more popular today than in the past (but it is difficult to substantiate this claim). It would be less than surprising in an age of Vietnam, urban ter-

---

* Hostile humor is not new; it can be traced back at least four or five centuries to the Punch and Judy puppet shows.

rorism, street crime, and guerilla sabotage, if people's minds were not focused on violence. Yet not everyone finds aggressive humor to their liking. While many are laughing at Don Rickles, there are others who are not.

Two issues can be raised here. The first deals with the content of humor over time, and the second deals with differences between people in response to a joke. The first rule of thumb for a comic is to make his humor topical, to tap the interests of the audience. A comedian would not tell jokes about air pollution to Fiji Islanders simply because they would not have the necessary background and experiences to comprehend such jokes. He would have to tell a joke that his audience could understand. Understanding, however, is not enough to make a joke funny. The joke would have to be one which the audience could relate to, one that would be involving and interesting to them. Our hypothetical comedian would be well-advised to tell medical jokes at a medical convention, political jokes at a legal meeting, and aggressive jokes to an audience familiar with, or concerned about, violence. In short, people most appreciate jokes whose content is familiar or salient to them. This conclusion is quite different from the explanation of the enjoyment of aggressive humor proposed by Freud and others. Freud proposed that people laugh at or tell aggressive (and sexual) jokes in order to relieve the tension and anxiety which these drives cause. He suggested that people appreciate aggressive jokes because society prohibits, and punishes, the free and indiscriminate expression of overt aggression. In order to prevent our aggression from building, we laugh at aggressive humor to keep our internal levels of aggression at some moderate, "safe" level.

In many experimental tests of this Freudian hypothesis, research subjects were exposed to aggressive or sexual stimuli which were designed to increase their internal levels of aggressive and sexual tension. Subjects then rated how funny they found aggressive, sexual, and "neutral" (nonsexual, nonaggressive) jokes. The Freudian hypothesis predicts that those who were aggressively aroused would prefer aggressive humor while those who were sexually aroused would prefer sexual humor. Most of these experimental tests supported this prediction.[52] There is in a sense a paradox resulting from this support: Are we to infer from the psychoanalytic hypothesis that those who find bowling jokes or medical jokes amusing have some internal drive or anxiety connected with these topics? That hardly seems reasonable, and to account for the appreciation of nonsexual, nonaggressive humor, Freud proposed a quite different explanation. A question which arises from this rather complicated state of affairs is whether it is necessary to account for aggressive and sexual humor appreciation in different terms from those used to explain appreciation of other types of humor. Ideally, a single set of explanatory principles would be used to account for all humor enjoyment. So, rather than starting from Freud in our quest to understand aggressive and other humor content, we may be better off starting from scratch.

Having dispensed for the moment with the psychoanalytic theory of humor, we can return to our initial problem: Why do some people appreciate aggressive humor? As I have hinted earlier, the familiarity or salience of a particular issue might be the key to its appreciation in humor. Just as the salience of violence makes violent film content preferred to other content, so salience of aggression or sex might serve to heighten the enjoyment of aggressive or sexual humor. In fact, whatever issues are salient to a person may lead to increased enjoyment of jokes revolving around those issues.

To test this hypothesis, Jerry Suls, Susan Anthony, and I embarked on a series of studies designed to determine the extent to which the notion of salience could account for enjoyment of specific types of humor content.[53] We followed, as closely as possible, the procedure which had been used to test the Freudian hypothesis. In one experiment, we exposed our research subjects, all college students, to photographs which depicted either scenes of violence and aggression or scenes of automobiles. Subjects then rated the funniness of cartoons which were either aggressive in nature or which centered on automobiles. According to predictions from psychoanalytic theory, only those subjects who had some internal aggressive drive, that is, the subjects exposed to aggressive photographs, would show a particular preference; they would seek to reduce their aggressive feelings by rating aggressive cartoons as most funny. The psychoanalytic theory would not be able to make any prediction concerning subjects exposed to automobile photographs; clearly, they should not experience any heightened tension or anxiety as a result of exposure to pictures of cars. On the other hand, the salience hypothesis predicts that whatever content area is most salient or familiar to a person will lead him to appreciate humor which centers on that particular topic. Thus, subjects exposed to aggressive pictures should most appreciate aggressive humor, while those first exposed to automobile pictures should most appreciate humor dealing with cars. The results of our studies clearly indicate support for the salience predictions. In several additional experiments designed to test the salience notion, including a cross-cultural test of the hypothesis in Africa and Japan, support was obtained in all cases. We were able to enhance the appreciation of medical and musical jokes merely by exposing subjects to stimuli of a medical or musical nature beforehand.[54]

In summary, appreciation for particular types of humor content is due largely to the salience or familiarity of that content to the humor recipient. We would expect that people to whom aggression is most familiar, say, residents of the inner city, as compared to those from the suburbs, would find aggressive humor most funny. As television has made realistic and almost instantaneous aggressive incidents available to all of us, as in coverage of the Vietnam War or the riots at political conventions, it follows that aggression and violence become more salient to us, and this increase in the prominence of violence would heighten our appreciation for aggressive humor. This does not mean that, because we may find aggressive humor funnier than in the past, we are ourselves more aggressive. Indeed, it may reflect our increased concern with violence rather than any increased propensity to engage in it.

MODELS IN THE PUBLIC EYE

Most of the topics discussed so far have focused on the learning of aggression and related norms in children. While behavior patterns of the child are likely to persist through adulthood, learning is a continual process and adults, too, are susceptible to the influence of rewards and punishments and of models in their social environment.

There are models in adults' environments which are for the most part absent from children's. In particular, people who have already achieved prominence by virtue of their wealth, status, or power are likely to serve as models for adults who aspire to wealth, status, or power.

Of singular importance to aggressive and criminal behavior would be models who have achieved some measure of success via illegitimate or aggressive means. For example, if a politician is exposed as having taken illegal contributions or kickbacks, as in the case of former Vice President Agnew, then those who aspire to be in a similar financial or social position become more likely to engage in illegal acts in order to achieve their goals. Successful criminals thus serve as reinforced models to observers. In addition, to the extent that such criminal models go unpunished, their illegal behavior becomes legitimized by society. If these arguments are correct, there should be an increase in criminality following disclosure of wrongdoing among political or public officials to the extent that the latter are seen as rewarded (for example, as wealthy) or to the extent that they go unpunished.

There are also more subtle cues legitimizing illegal acts. For example, in many cities throughout America, cars prominently display stickers or tags indicating support for the police. One reason—albeit an implicit one—for such display is as a sign to the police to deal leniently with the driver of the car in cases of il-legal parking and other traffic offenses. On one level, the tags imply—whether correctly or not—that the law is flexible, that it applies, or should apply, more fully to some people than to others.

This chapter has examined a number of factors associated with an individual's chronic level of aggression. Perhaps the most suc-cinct summary of this was given by Fredric Wertham: "Violence is as contagious as the measles."[55]

SITUATIONAL FACTORS ASSOCIATED WITH AGGRESSION

3

Many people are capable of homicide or assault whose earlier experiences could not be distinguished from those of the law abiding.

William Goode[1]

If it is true, as has been proposed, that most Americans (or most people who share any culture) have the same approximate modal levels of aggression, then most violence can be accounted for in terms of situational factors. This is a fairly startling assertion in view of the fact that so much attention has been devoted in the past to an examination of "criminal personalities" and child-rearing correlates of aggression. The situational approach to aggression and crime assumes that, among people who have learned at least some aggressive behaviors, personality and early childhood experiences play only a minor role in the causation of violent acts. Of utmost importance in aggression are factors present in the situation immediately preceding the act.[2] If the situation is not appropriate, if aggressive weapons and targets are not available, no aggression will occur. To stress situational and environmental variables is to ask whether anyone, given "appropriate" circumstances, might not behave criminally or aggressively. As in James Dickey's novel, *Deliverance,* average middle-class men, to whom violence is quite alien, may, in certain situations, commit murder.

In order to demonstrate the importance of situational factors in violence, a brief summary of statistical findings on criminal homicide is presented below. This survey includes information about the nature of homicide in terms of time and place, victim-offender relationships, motives, and means.

THE CASE OF CRIMINAL HOMICIDE

In his pioneering study of homicide, the criminologist Marvin Wolfgang, of the University of Pennsylvania, presented a detailed examination of the 588 criminal homicides which occurred in Philadelphia between the years 1948 and 1952.[3]

Motives

In those cases where the offender's motives could be determined, the greatest motive precipitating homicide consisted of relatively trivial insults, curses, threats, and jostlings. These trivial motives accounted for 37 per cent of all ascertainable motives. (Likewise, in Great Britain the number of homicides committed for relatively inconsequential, personal motives far exceeds those committed for criminal motives and homicides committed by persons considered "abnormal."[4])

Victim-Offender Relationships and Environmental Factors

Fully one-half of the 588 homicides analyzed by Wolfgang occurred between a victim and an offender who were friends or relatives. One hundred of the homicides involved the slaying of the offender's spouse. In only about 13 per cent of the cases were the victim and offender unacquainted with one another prior to the crime.

If homicides are examined in terms of their relative brutality (brutal or violent homicides are defined by Wolfgang as those involving two or more gun shots or stabbings, or beatings resulting in death), a number of intriguing results are obtained. First, whites were slightly, but not significantly, more violent than Negroes in the commission of homicides. Forty-six per cent of the men and 63 per cent of the women victims were killed violently. Homicides occurring in the homes of the victims and/or offenders were significantly more likely to be violent than those which occurred outside the home. Spouse slayings were significantly more violent than those for any other type of interpersonal relationship between victim and offender.

With regard to the location of homicides, it was found that for women offenders homicide was most likely to occur in the home (80 per cent of the cases). In fact, a female who committed homicide was apt to have done so in the kitchen (29 per cent) or bedroom (26 per cent) of her own home. Male offenders committed homicide in their homes 45 per cent of the time and on public streets or property 35 per cent of the time. A man who did commit homicide in his home was most likely to have done so in the bedroom or living room and least likely to have done so in the kitchen or on the stairway.

In 94 per cent of the homicide cases, the victim and offender were of the same race. (In the 6 per cent which crossed racial boundaries, about half of the victims were black and about half were white.)

For female offenders, the weapon most often used was a knife (in 64 per cent of the female cases), while for male offenders a pistol or revolver was the most commonly used weapon (in 27 per cent of the male cases).

The victims of homicide tended to be older than their murderers and, in general, the young—those under thirty-five years of age—tended to be overrepresented among offenders.

Alcohol and Homicide

One of the strongest associations found in the Wolfgang study was the relationship between the presence of alcohol in the victim or offender and homicide. In nearly two-thirds of the 588 cases, the victim, the offender, or both had been drinking just prior to the murder.

Time

Although there were no statistically significant differences between the months of the year, over 55 per cent of the homicides were committed during the warmer months (April through September). Nearly two-thirds of the homicides occurred on Friday, Saturday, and Sunday, and half the homicides occurred between the hours of 8 P.M. and 2 A.M. (These are also the days and times during which most alcohol is consumed.)

A number of studies conducted at different times and in different locations have provided evidence which corroborates the findings obtained by Wolfgang.[5] Former Attorney General Ramsey Clark, for example, has estimated that "two-thirds of all aggravated assaults occur within a family or among neighbors or friends," and Amir has reported that rape is most often committed by someone acquainted with his victim.[6]

The aspects of the above findings which point to the importance of causes of violence which are more or less independent of the personality of the offender will now be examined in terms of the situational conditions which underlie them.

THE ROLE OF SITUATIONAL FACTORS IN VIOLENCE

Motives

Some have expanded the finding that the motives which lay behind homicide are relatively trivial to suggest that while the motive may seem trivial, it is actually a disguise for some more deeply rooted cause. Others have seen in this result evidence for the accumulation of frustrations; they have argued that an insult or minor threat could not actually be considered the cause of so serious an event. They say that the offenders have been carrying with them a reservoir of earlier frustrations which, added to the minor insult or threat, become too much for them to bear. Still others have suggested that what may seem minor insults and threats to outside observers may in fact be perceived as major assaults on the offender's self-esteem. All of these explanations have in common a focus on some internal characteristic of the offender. However, rather than examining personality dynamics in an attempt to explain why minor events trigger homicide, a more fruitful search can be conducted by examining other environmental variables which are present in the homicide situation.

Victim-Offender Relationships: The Role of Similarity and Familiarity in Violence

The most outstanding feature of Wolfgang's analysis is the many ways in which familiarity and similarity manifest themselves. Offenders and victims are most likely to be familiar with one another prior to the homicide; the homicide is most likely to occur in a place familiar to the offender; the weapon is usually familiar to the offender. The most intimate, familiar relationship which two people can share—marriage—accounted not only for a large proportion of all homicides, but also tended to be the victim-offender relationship which contained the most violence and brutality. Rape also tends to occur in an environment familiar to the offender, against a victim familiar to the offender. And even the looting of stores during a riot will most likely take place in those establishments with which the looters are most familiar.[7]

The most striking implication of these findings is that people with whom one interacts most often in a positive, friendly manner are also those toward whom one will interact most violently under provocation. This leads us to the idea that there may be something in the nature of friendship, other than the mere fact that friends spend more time in contact than strangers, which increases the probability that aggression will occur.

You Always Hurt the One You Love: A hypothesis may be proposed that as a person becomes increasingly familiar with another, the probability that he or she will aggress against the

other will also increase. Although the statistics generated by
Wolfgang, Amir, and others, bear this out, no satisfactory explanation for this effect has been provided.

There are a number of possible explanations for the finding
that aggression is more probable toward a familiar victim. According to an interpretation based on the psychoanalytic school
of thought, the formation of positive emotional bonds with another involves a giving up of some autonomy and freedom; the
stronger the positive bonds, the more individuality must be sacrificed. Therefore, relationships between people tend to be am-
bivalent, and the extent of ambivalence is directly related to the
amount of attraction they feel toward one another. As the positive affect between two people increases, so does the negative
affect. If positive interaction between the two is fairly intense,
negative interaction as during an argument, will be equally
strong. What is suggested here is that the *intensity* of interaction
between any two people is relatively constant, while the *quality*
of the affect, either positive or negative, changes with the circumstances. For example, positive interaction with a recent ac-
quaintance might involve a handshake, a smile, and some casual
conversation, while negative interaction with the same person
might take the form of a mild insult or sneer. With a close friend
or relative, however, positive interaction generally involves sharing secrets or objects and close physical contact. When one
wishes to express disapproval of such a person, it will be done
in an intense fashion, as by a strong verbal attack or by physical
injury.

Another explanation can be given in terms of the principles
proposed earlier: the familiarity-aggression effect can be seen as
a conflict of values and norms. Nearly everyone in Western society learns contradictory norms and values for assertion and
aggression and for control and restraint. In the presence of familiar others (or in a familiar physical environment), people act
less defensively and do not censor their behavior to the extent
that they do in the presence of strangers (or in unfamiliar sur-

roundings). In other words, people are more likely to act impulsively and are less likely to inhibit themselves in the presence of close friends and relatives. Therefore, given a relatively mild provocation, people are more apt to respond aggressively toward friends than toward strangers, and in a familiar than an unfamiliar setting.

It is also possible that in familiar places a mild insult or threat will seem greater than it would otherwise. This can be due to the fact that a familiar environment, by virtue of its familiarity, does not intrude very much on a person's consciousness; there are few if any novel features in a familiar environment to hold one's attention. A mild insult may be exaggerated because it stands out from the relatively unobtrusive environment. In a novel environment, the insult may seem less intense since it must compete with other novel features of the environment for one's attention.

Not only are people more likely to aggress in familiar environments, but they are more likely to take actions of any kind. In research on altruism, it has been found that people were more quick to help a person in distress in familiar than in unfamiliar environments. In terms of the aggression model presented in Chapter 1, these results suggest that pro-helping norms will be acted upon more quickly in a familiar environment because inhibitory, anti-helping norms are relatively weak in such situations. This aspect of the aggression model is discussed more fully by Goldstein, Davis, and Herman, and by Latané and Darley.[8]

Even though it is possible to explain why crimes of violence are more likely against friends and relatives than strangers, and why such crimes tend to be more brutal than those committed against others, it is difficult to imagine how people who are normally affectionate toward one another can, in a relatively short time, become violent and brutal. In order to resolve this paradox it will be necessary to examine some of the cognitive dynamics which are proposed to operate in aggressive encounters.

The Cognitive Consequences of Aggressing. When we are familiar and friendly with others, we develop positive attitudes toward them, and our expectations about their behavior are raised in the sense that we anticipate our interactions with them to be pleasurable and psychologically rewarding. When such people anger, insult, or disappoint us, one of our initial impulses is likely to be aggression or retaliation in kind. Therefore, when we are provoked by our friends, a conflict is experienced between our normally favorable attitudes and behaviors toward them and aggressive tendencies toward them.

This is a difficult conflict to resolve. After all, we would not become friendly or intimate with people who were not pleasing to us. When they anger or otherwise provoke us, we have to weigh the consequences of our impulsive, aggressive tendencies against the long-range effects such aggression might have. We may wish to hurt them in retaliation, but at the same time not lose their friendship. In most such situations, the conflict is resolved by nonviolent means: the individual decides either that aggression would be too costly or inappropriate or that his or her positive feelings toward the other person outweigh the immediately felt negative feelings. In some cases, however, the conflict is resolved by violent means. Aggression is most apt to be used in such a situation when the person provoked is in a familiar environment or has a weapon readily at hand.

Let us assume that aggression has already occurred, that Person A has aggressed against his friend, Person B. At this point, there still may be some residual conflict, wherein A retains in his mind positive feelings toward B. Having already aggressed, A must now justify his actions to himself. He is likely to reevaluate B, adding reasons to justify his (A's) aggression and minimizing his feelings of friendliness toward B. (Likewise, if, in such a conflict situation, the individual decides not to aggress even though he may be provoked, he will also think of justifications for this decision. Because of this justification, it is not unusual for verbal disagreements to end in a reconciliation in which both parties feel closer to one another than prior to the dispute.)

When aggression occurs there is a general tendency to devalue the victim of the attack. This devaluation may be successful enough to warrant even further attacks, each with attendant
devaluations of the victim. In this way, a general increase in the
amount or intensity of aggression will occur. The paradox of in-
ordinate amounts of violence being perpetrated against friends
and relatives can be resolved by recognizing the need of the aggressor to justify his or her actions, usually by devaluing the victim. Those victims requiring the greatest amounts of devaluation
are friends and relatives, and those provocations which neces-
sitate maximum devaluation of the victim tend to be the trivial
ones. With successful devaluation, additional amounts of violence become easier to administer.

The consequences of aggression in terms of devaluation of the
victim are widespread. On an international level, nations devalue
enemies in times of war; within societies, the poor and the jobless,
the sick and the needy are frequently devalued. Melvin Lerner[9]
has proposed a theory on the psychological devaluation of such
victims of circumstance which he calls the "just world phenomenon." According to Lerner, people have a need to believe
that events in the world are not unjust, fortuitous, meaningless,
or random, but that things happen to people as a result of some
orderly and logical process of causality. The need to believe that
the world is an orderly place leads to some surprising inferences.
If the world is orderly, then things happen to people because of
their own efforts. The Protestant ethic clearly implies this. Therefore, good things should not happen to people who are bad, nor
should bad things happen to those who are good. Most people
probably think of themselves as honest, righteous, and moral,
and when material or psychological ills befall them, it is difficult
for them to understand. After all, bad things should not happen
to them since they do not consider themselves deserving of any
such "punishment." I venture to guess that the most common
prayer is "Why me, God?" (followed closely by "What have I
done to deserve this?").

If we observe good or bad things happening to others there is a tendency to look for explanations; and if people look hard enough, they will find—or fabricate—them. Reasons and causes for events serve to strengthen belief in the justness and orderliness of the world. The unemployed are seen as out of work because they are "lazy"; slum-dwellers live in rundown housing because they are "sloppy"; the poor have too many children because they are "oversexed"; women are raped because they wear immodest clothing. All of these "explanations" serve to sustain the belief that the world is just. People, in other words, not only are believed to get what they deserve but also to deserve what they get.

An experiment by Jones and Aronson[10] found that the more respectable the victim of a rape, the greater the fault attributed to her for the incident. College students were presented with a description of a rape, the victim being described either as a virgin, as married, or as divorced. When asked how much they considered the rape to be the fault of the victim, students attributed greatest fault to the married woman and least to the divorced woman. These results suggest that it is more difficult to understand and justify the rape of a married woman or a virgin, and in order to maintain their beliefs in a just world, the subjects of the study assigned the greatest responsibility to these victims.

With regard to aggression, when we observe a victim of violence, there is a tendency to justify his or her victimization, no less so if we are the perpetrators of that violence. If we aggress against someone, particularly if it is difficult to justify such aggression, there will be a tendency to devalue the victim, to attribute fault to the victim for our own acts of aggression. One area in which this can be seen is child abuse.

The Battered Child.   Child abuse is the excessive use of physical punishment against children. Rates of child abuse (per 100,000 children under 18 years of age) range from a high of 31.2 in Texas to nearly zero in Rhode Island and South Dakota. In a nationwide survey Gil found that the median child abuse rate for the United States as a whole was approximately 4.4 per

100,000 children.[11] It is likely, however, that many, if not most, of the child abuse cases go unreported and undetected by official agencies. It has been pointed out that child abuse is not widespread enough in this country to be considered a *major* social problem,[12] but it is a disturbing event and certainly serves to highlight and dramatize the violence which many people are capable of committing.

In his national survey, Gil found that over 58 per cent of his respondents agreed with the statement that "almost anybody could at some time injure a child in his care," and over 22 per cent agreed that they themselves "could at some time injure a child." Those who engage in child abuse may not be very different psychologically from normal, nonabusing parents. In a study of sixty abusing parents, Steele and Pollock[13] noted: "If all the people we studied were gathered together, they would not seem much different than a group picked by stopping the first dozen people one would meet on a downtown street."

A number of explanations have been proposed to account for child abuse, and particularly what has been called the "battered child syndrome" by C. H. Kempe and his colleagues at the University of Colorado School of Medicine.[14] The majority of these explanations are psychoanalytic in origin and emphasis. For example, Morris, Gould, and Matthews[15] have stated that an abusing parent views his victim not only as a child but also as his own parent who has failed, hurt, and frustrated him. A related interpretation is that the parent has a great deal of self-hatred and that, particularly in cases where the child resembles the parent, it is "taken out" on the child. A prevalent explanation of child abuse is that the child fails to live up to the expectations of the parents, and the parents, continually frustrated by the child's inability to perform adequately, punish it for its shortcomings. (This interpretation is not dissimilar to one based on frustration-aggression theory.[16])

Since experimental data on child abuse are virtually nonexistent and official statistics probably unreliable, there is no sufficiently testable theory for the battered child phenomenon.

Also, the relationship between child abuse and other forms of aggression is unknown. An important issue is whether beating one's own children is qualitatively different from other forms of aggression such as homicide, assault, and rape. Obviously, it is easiest in discussing aggression not to make distinctions unless they are warranted by available data or commanded by existing theory. In their absence, however, it might be most prudent to consider child abuse as one kind of human aggression which is governed by the same set of principles as other forms of aggression.

If this is so, we can speculate on some of the dynamics of child abuse. A necessary condition is a parent who has learned some basic aggressive responses. As mentioned above, almost all Americans have had such aggression training, and therefore we are led to conclude that, under appropriate circumstances, almost any American parent is capable of battering his or her own child. This conclusion agrees with the results of Gil's survey in which a cross-section of Americans believed this to be the case. Second, we would need a parent who experiences conflict about aggressing toward the child. That is, some provocation to aggress (negative or hostile feelings) must be salient along with positive feelings toward the child. A third step in child abuse would involve the decision to actually strike the child. Succeeding stages would involve the cognitive devaluation of the child, which would justify even further aggression. With each act of aggression, the child is further devalued, justifying the need for additional aggression.

In order to test these ideas, a series of experiments by Goldstein, Davis, and Herman[17] were conducted at Temple University. The first experiment involved pairs of college students, one of whom was to reward or punish the other for responses on a learning task. Some students could punish the other with any of ten verbal statements ranging from mild ("That's no good.") to strong ("Stupid son of a bitch.") each time he made a mistake. Other students could use any of ten levels of reward, ranging from mild ("Yes.") to strong ("That's fantastic!") for correct answers to the learning task. Each of the students administered twenty rewards or twenty punishments to the learner. Following the learning task, the "teachers" were asked to evaluate the learners on cooperativeness, likeability, and intelligence. What we expected was that subjects would find it increasingly easy to give severe verbal punishments to the learner as the experiment progressed. We also expected that this increased punishment would be accompanied by a general devaluation of the learner; this is precisely what we found. As students administered verbal punishments to the learner, the intensity of the punishment increased. In addition, subjects who punished the learner rated him significantly less cooperative, friendly, and likeable than those who rewarded the learner.*

In a second experiment, some learners (who were actually accomplices of the experimenters) improved their learning performance as the study progressed, while other learners did not improve. Again, half the subjects in the experiment could reward the learner with varying degrees of reward for correct answers on the learning task, while the remaining half could punish the learner with varying degrees of verbal punishment for errors on the task. We found that, regardless of the performance of the learner, subjects gave increasingly intense punishment to the learner as the learning task progressed. The results of this study are shown in Figure 3.1.

These experiments suggest, first, that normal people can become quite hostile with little or no apparent provocation, second, that it becomes increasingly easy to escalate the level of verbal aggression, third, that increasing verbal aggression is often accompanied by a general devaluation of the "victim," finally, these behaviors were found to occur regardless of the performance of the learner. This last finding suggests that once aggression is underway, it may operate in a fairly automatic fashion, independently of the behavior of the victim. This find-

---

* It should be noted that those subjects who rewarded correct responses also showed an escalation, giving increasing intensity of reward as the learning task progressed. This is discussed further in Chapter 4.

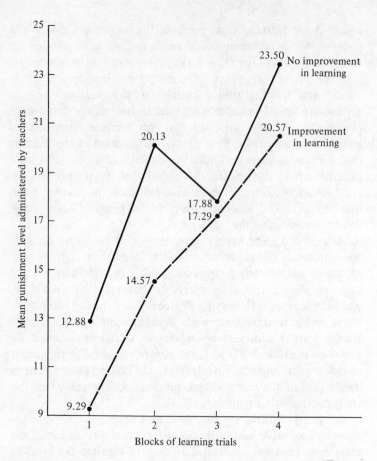

Figure 3.1. Escalation of aggression. Adapted from Goldstein, Davis, and Herman.

ing has also been reported in other research.[18] It is not surprising in view of these results that following an argument or fight, the participants often cannot remember what the dispute was about. At some point the act of arguing or aggressing becomes autonomous and is done for its own sake. One reason for this may be that highly intense verbal or physical assault becomes self-reinforcing and may have an almost hypnotic effect wherein the actor loses awareness of his or her surroundings.

THE EFFECTS OF PHYSIOLOGICAL CHANGES

Aggression is an act which requires at least a minimal amount of physical energy to perform. We might expect that if a person has already decided to engage in aggressive behavior, the more energy he or she has available (that is, the more aroused the person is), the more intense will be the aggression.* An increasing number of research reports indicate that rise in arousal level usually leads to an increase in aggression, at least among those who are required to aggress as part of their experimental participation.[19] In most of these studies, it makes little difference whether the source of the research subjects' heightened state of arousal is due to injected adrenalin,[20] to sexually stimulating pictures,[21] to increased emotionality or frustration,[22] or to unpleasant arousing noise.[23]

The evidence is strongest for the relationship between sexual arousal and aggressiveness; an increase in one's level of sex arousal is generally followed by an increase in level of aggressiveness. A. M. Barclay,[24] for example, found that subjects who were sexually aroused became more aggressive following their arousal, but that those who were aroused as a result of observing a slapstick comedy did not become more aggressive. A possible reason why there might be a close relationship between sex and aggression is based on the fact that brain centers which are capable of evoking sexual and aggressive behaviors are located anatomically close to one another. Another reason, based on psychoanalytic theory, is the fact that both sexual and aggressive behaviors are closely regulated by society.[25] Not enough research has been conducted to warrant drawing any conclusions about the precise relationship between sex and aggression, however.

There are environmental characteristics, such as crowding

* This will be true providing the amount of energy is not so high as to debilitate the individual.

and temperature extremes, which are often thought to influence aggression by first raising the individual's level of physiological arousal. Interest in the effects of crowding on human aggression can be traced to the well-known studies of J. B. Calhoun,[26] who found that rats reared in crowded conditions developed abnormal behavior patterns, including hyperaggressiveness. Research on human population density and aggression has been less than consistent. This is due in part to the difficulties of researching the topic with humans. If a researcher compares the rate of violent crime in a high population density area, such as Harlem, with that of a low population density area, such as Westchester County, New York, he is likely to find a significant difference; but this cannot be attributed to differences in population density, since Harlem and Westchester also differ in a variety of other ways, any one of which might account for variations in the crime rate. An alternative strategy to this correlational approach is to place some research subjects in crowded conditions and others in uncrowded conditions and then compare their relative rates of aggressiveness. While this is the strategy most often followed by psychologists, short-term crowding may not have the same effects as long-term crowding.

Comparative crime statistics for urban (crowded) and rural (uncrowded) areas within the United States, as well as other countries, indicate uniformly that there is more crime in the cities than in the hinterlands. In 1971, the rate of violent crime in United States cities of over 250,000 inhabitants was 1047 per 100,000 people, while in suburban areas the rate was 206 and in rural areas 133 per 100,000 people.[27] This relationship, however, may be explained on the basis of variables other than crowding. The effects of laboratory experiments on crowding and aggression generally have not reported an increase in aggressiveness as a result of short-term crowding.[28] Thus, if crowding does influence human aggression, it does so either by first influencing other aspects of the individual or only after a long period of time.

Situational Factors Associated with Aggression 77

Philip Zimbardo and others[29] have suggested that the effects of crowding may be to influence the individual's feelings of identity or anonymity and that this might account for changes in aggression. Individuals in densely or heavily populated places may feel less unique, less visible, and because of this, less accountable for their actions. They may, therefore, behave more impulsively and violently than they would otherwise. While Zimbardo has conducted research which supports the hypothesis that individuals who do not feel strongly identifiable or "individuated" behave more aggressively, it is possible that these effects are less than universal. In Tokyo, Japan, for example, where the population density is higher than in New York City and where there are 12 million people, there were 213 murders in 1970, compared to 1,117 in New York City (where the population is about 8 million).[30] In general, it would seem that population density per se has little direct influence on human aggression, although it may at times influence aggression through indirect means.

One well-known criminological finding is that the southern areas of many countries (for example, the United States and Italy) have higher rates of violent crime than northern areas. It has often been thought that this might be the case because temperature somehow influenced aggressiveness. However, the relationship between temperature and aggression has been investigated in only a few studies, and in most of them there was no direct relationship between the two variables.[31] A study by Baron and Lawton[32] did find that increased temperature led to greater imitation of an aggressive model, but that subjects who did not observe a model were not more aggressive in warm than in cool temperatures.

"Old Times There Are Not Forgotten."
The greater violence rate found in the southern section of the United States than in the northern has been examined by Gastil.[33] The homicide rate for 1971 was 12.2 per 100,000 people in the southern states, nearly twice the rate reported for the

northern, north central, and western states, all of whose homicide rates were less than 7.0 per 100,000. Gastil proposed that the higher rate in the south was because of the cultural tradition of violence there: people more often carry weapons, attempt to redress insults to personal honor, and only infrequently receive punishment for violence. By tracing migration patterns of southerners to nonsouthern states, Gastil was able to account for a significant portion of the homicide rates of all states. The homicide rate for any given state was highly related to the proportion of southerners or descendants of southerners in the state's population, although other variables such as education and income also account for large proportions of the homicide rates. If we can carry Gastil's thesis one step further, the southern tradition of violence might also partially explain the relatively greater rate of violent crime among black than among white Americans, although here again other factors, including education and income, undoubtedly play a large role.[34] Of importance to our discussion of environmental variables is the fact that the greater rate of violence in the south is unrelated to such factors as weather and temperature.

Effects of Alcohol and Drugs

One finding common to many investigations of violent crime, both in the United States and abroad, is the great number of people who commit offenses while under the influence of alcohol. Wolfgang found that of 588 cases of criminal homicide, alcohol was present in at least 64 per cent of them, and he reports the results of other studies indicating a strong relationship between alcohol and violent crime in England, Norway, Ukraina, and Yugoslavia.[35] Shupe[36] reported that 91 of 100 people arrested for assault or for carrying a concealed weapon showed evidence of alcohol intake.

Experimental studies with human research subjects on the effects of alcohol on aggression do not always lead to consistent results. Bennett, Buss, and Carpenter[37] gave their research subjects varying quantities of vodka and found no differences in aggressiveness with changes in vodka dosage. On the other hand, Shuntich and Taylor[38] found that subjects drunk on bourbon were significantly more aggressive than those given no drugs or a placebo. The inconsistency between these results might be resolved by making distinctions between different kinds of alcoholic components contained in commercial liquor.

Besides containing ethanol, alcoholic beverages contain a number of ketones and esters which used to be referred to as *fusel oils* but which are now grouped together under the label of *congeners*. There are a number of congeners in commercial alcoholic beverages including acetaldehyde, ethyl formate, ethyl acetate, and methanol. Different alcoholic beverages contain varying amounts of these substances, with bourbon containing the most congeners and vodka the least.[39] In between bourbon and vodka, increasing amounts of congeners are found in Canadian whiskey, scotch, brandy, rum, and rye. A number of studies using both animal and human subjects have reported an increase in aggressiveness or risk-taking as a result, not only of alcohol dosage but of congener dosage.[40] However, the effects of congeners themselves are not always predictable, since there are some studies in the literature which report that increasing the level of congeners had no appreciable effect on aggression or social behavior.[41] Since congeners consist of a variety of substances, it is conceivable that one or more of these, such as acetaldehyde or methanol, are responsible for increased aggression.

While congeners, or some types of congener, may lead to increases in aggression, not everyone who drinks heavily becomes violent. Aggression would be greatest when the organism is moderately aroused rather than over- or under-aroused, providing that the person has already decided on aggressive behavior. In fact, on a purely physiological level, a good case can be made that only moderate amounts of alcohol (or congeners) are positively related to aggression, since excessive amounts are likely to impair motor performance and render the intoxicated person relatively harmless. The hypothesis that alcohol may be related to aggression in a curvilinear rather than a linear way has been supported in a study by Peeke, Ellman, and Herz.*[42]

Also of importance in understanding the effects of alcohol (or other drugs) on aggression are a variety of social factors. The effects which alcoholic beverages have on consumers are in part determined by the expectations which the drinkers have; and people's expectations about the effects of alcohol are learned primarily in family interactions. Among the Irish, whose per capita consumption of alcohol is high, lethal violence "under the influence" is a rare occurrence; among Jews, whose consumption of alcohol is imbedded in religious tradition, both alcoholism and alcohol-related violence are infrequent.

Alcohol is medically classified as a depressant which acts to inhibit activity of the central nervous system. This "inhibition system" is both cognitive and physiological. In Western society alcohol is often used as a stimulant (a drink is often referred to as a "pick-me-up" in the United States) and as a social lubricant. That a drug which dulls the senses can be perceived as heightening sensitivity points to the importance of expectations in drug effects. Indeed, marihuana can be perceived by users as either heightening arousal or decreasing arousal, depending on the expectations and learning experiences of the user.[43] We might even hypothesize that some people drink in order to become more aggressive, and if they expect alcohol to make them violent, it will. This can also serve as an excuse for aggression,

---

* Male convict cichlid fish were placed in tanks with .07, .18, or .33 per cent ethanol and, after several hours, another male cichlid in a glass tube was suspended in the tank. Attacks were most ferocious and more frequent among fish in the 18 per cent solution. It is conceivable that comparable effects would obtain for aggression and arousal in humans. A problem raised by these findings and by the hypothesis that arousal is curvilinearly related to aggression is that boredom (lack of stimulation) as well as overstimulation are known to be aversive states for man and animals. One consequence of over- and under-stimulation is often aggression. It is for this reason that I have qualified the curvilinear hypothesis by stating that moderate arousal will lead to maximum aggression only among those already motivated to aggress.

since the aggressor can absolve himself or herself of responsibility by blaming his or her behavior on liquor.

A physiological explanation to account for the fact that alcohol is a depressant but aggression is heightened as a result of intoxication is that alcohol (or congeners) serves to depress those mental and physical aspects of an individual which operate to inhibit aggressive behavior. In other words, alcohol inhibits the aggression inhibition systems, thus making aggression more likely.

Most drugs consumed by large numbers of people generally have little direct effect on aggression level. In a review of drug effects it was noted that marihuana, LSD-25, mescaline, psilocybin, heroin, morphine, opium, codeine, methadone, and the barbiturates generally did not lead to an increase in aggressiveness.[44] Of all the drugs reviewed, only amphetamines and alcohol were found to be related to an increase in aggression, with the evidence for the alcohol-aggression relationship being strongest.

There is considerable evidence that a substantial proportion of street crime, particularly robbery and auto theft, is caused by the excessive need for money experienced by heroin addicts. For example, it has been estimated that in the city of Philadelphia alone, the approximately ten thousand heroin addicts must steal nearly one-half billion dollars' worth of goods a year to support their drug addiction.[45] This problem is discussed in Chapter 5, but it should be noted here that the evidence for heightened aggression due to heroin addiction per se is weak or nonexistent.

THE AVAILABILITY OF WEAPONS AND VIOLENCE

Americans are armed to a greater extent than the peoples of any other nation on earth.[46] One-half of all American homes have at least one lethal weapon, and there are estimated to be 90,000,000 rifles, handguns, and shotguns in the hands of civilians.[47] In 1967, there were nearly three thousand accidental deaths from firearms, eight thousand homicides, seventy thousand robberies, and fifty thousand aggravated assaults. Guns were used as the murder weapon in 96 per cent of the killings of policemen from 1960-68. Morris and Hawkins report that "since the beginning of this century some three-quarters of a million people have been killed in the United States by privately owned guns, 30 per cent more than in all the wars in which this country has been involved in its entire history."[48]

The homicide rates in those states with strict gun control laws are significantly lower than in those states with weak gun laws. Likewise, homicides and suicides by firearm are significantly lower in those countries with strict gun laws than in those without strict laws (see Figure 3.2).

There are a number of ways in which the presence of weapons can lead to increased violence. A well-known and controversial experiment by L. Berkowitz and A. LePage[49] of the University of Wisconsin found that the mere presence of a weapon during an aggression experiment could intensify the level of electric shock which subjects would administer to another person.[50] Berkowitz has stated that "guns not only permit violence, they can stimulate it as well. The finger pulls the trigger, but the trigger may also be pulling the finger."[51] The possession of a weapon, even though its owner is reluctant or forbidden to use it, may increase the intensity of other forms of violence.[52] In a society in which so many people are armed, the assumption that an opponent may be carrying a weapon often leads to the notion that it is better to "shoot first and ask questions later." Finally, as Morris and Hawkins[53] have stated, "it is most implausible to assume that the individuals involved in the majority of murder cases are persons so determined to kill that in the absence of guns they will either seek to achieve that purpose with any available alternative or deliberately evade whatever restrictive gun legislation may be enacted. . . . Without the vehicle there is every reason to expect the violence to be both less lethal and less injurious."

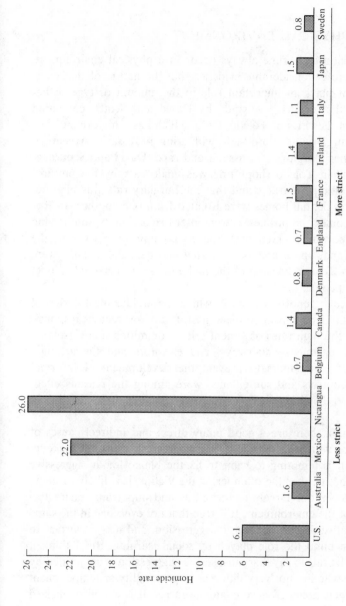

Figure 3.2. Homicide rate for countries with less and more strict gun control laws than the United States. The homicide rate is expressed per 100,000 population. Rating of gun control laws was adapted from G. D. Newton and F. E. Zimring. *Firearms and violence in American life.* Washington, D.C.: U.S. Government Printing Office, 1969.

THE PHYSICAL ENVIRONMENT

Aggression and crime always occur in a physical environment, and there is considerable evidence that the nature of that environment plays an important role in the amount or type of behavior that occurs.[54] A study by David and Scott[55] compared crime in the cities of Toledo, Ohio, which has a high rate of larceny, burglary, and auto theft, with crime in Rosario, Argentina, which has a high rate of assault and rape. David and Scott suggest that in Toledo shoplifting was made easy by the physical layout of supermarkets and that the burglary rate was high because residential homes were isolated from one another. In Rosario, homes and businesses were intermixed, thereby minimizing the opportunity and temptation to commit burglary. On the other hand, opportunities for sexual and personal assaults were great in Rosario because of the high amount of personal contact among people.

Yancey[56] reports a study in which the architectural design of the Pruitt-Igoe housing project in St. Louis was seen as responsible for the high rates of violent crime committed there. Isolated doors, apartments, stairways, and elevators and the arrangement of living units to prevent the development of informal social controls and surveillance were among the reasons cited. It is also the case that most stolen cars have had the keys left in them.

In sum, there are a good many direct and indirect causes of violence which lie outside of the aggressor's personal makeup. While it is tempting to want to fix the blame for an aggressive episode on either the offender or the victim, it is likely in many cases to be due largely to fortuitous and impersonal characteristics of the environment. It is true that not everyone in the same physical setting will engage in aggression, and it is important to keep in mind the role played by social learning. But I think it would be fair to say that most serious aggression is committed by people who are not very different in personality or temperament from their nonaggressive contemporaries. It is a well-publicized fact that many people arrested for serious offenses have records of previous arrests. Most of these people belong to violent subcultures and inhabit environments which foster illegal conduct, or are desperate for money to support a heroin addiction. Such multiple offenders tend not to be involved in violent attacks on others but have long histories of arrests for misdemeanors, forgery, and property crimes. A considerable amount of violent crime is committed by first offenders—people who were in the wrong place with the wrong people under the wrong circumstances.

FACTORS ASSOCIATED WITH NONAGGRESSION

Absolute morality is the regulation of conduct in such a way that pain shall not be inflicted.

Herbert Spencer[1]

In many instances, the mere absence of aggression-provoking factors is sufficient to preclude aggressive action. For example, in the absence of any kind of arousal, with no available target of aggression and with no available weaponry aggressive behavior will be most unlikely to occur. And there are situations and processes, both internal and external to the individual, which tend to minimize the likelihood of aggressive behavior. Before looking at such nonaggression variables, a closer examination of aggression conflict is made in order to see more clearly how nonaggression factors operate within the larger model of aggression.

The decision of whether or not to act aggressively is a complex one involving a large number of units and subprocesses. The aggression model proposed in the first chapter stated that aggression will ensue when the sum of the long-term and situational factors associated with aggression is seen as stronger or more potent by the individual than the sum of long-term and situational factors associated with nonaggression. The individual in essence uses a kind of cognitive arithmetic to determine which of the two sets of competing behavioral tendencies is strongest, and his or her actions reflect this cognitive judgment. Of course, this decision-making process occurs relatively quickly, probably in a matter of a few seconds, and is most often not entirely conscious.

In situations in which one side of the equation (either the pro- or the anti-aggression side) is predominant, the behavior in which the individual will engage is quite easily determined. However, when the balance of opposing forces is nearly even, the individual must weigh more closely each aspect of the entire situation. He must decide how angered or upset he really is, how just or unjust aggression would be in that situation, how powerful his opponent is, how characteristic he believes aggressive behavior to be of his own personality, and so on. We have seen that an individual is capable of distorting his perceptions of the potential victim, and he is equally capable of distorting his perceptions of any other aspect of a potential aggression situation. Therefore, while it is possible to determine somewhat objectively how most people view various provocations, victims, and situations, it should be clear that these factors may be weighted and evaluated differently by different people and that the outcome is influenced by subjective factors such as psychological distortion. In cases where the pro- and anti-aggression forces are felt to be of roughly equal intensity by an individual, we can speak of a high conflict situation. High conflict situations require considerably more cognitive arithmetic to resolve than low conflict situations simply because it is more difficult to justify one action over another. (See Figure 4.1.)

For some people aggression is never an easy behavior in which to engage; it is seen as morally wrong, inefficient, or unjustified. For others aggression may be seen as useful, appropriate, and rewarding. The kinds of factors associated with the former norms will be considered below. Just as there are two

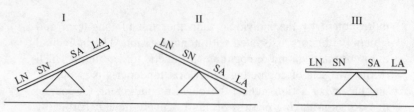

Figure 4.1. Aggression conflict. In I the short-term and long-term aggression factors are outweighed by the short-term and long-term nonaggression factors, so nonaggressive behavior will result. In II, the aggression factors outweigh the nonaggression factors, so aggression will result. In III, they are about equal, so it is unclear which type of behavior will ultimately be expressed. In the last condition, the individual will have to evaluate closely each element in the situation before deciding which behavior to engage in. (LN = long-term nonaggression factors; SN = short-term nonaggression factors; SA = short-term pro-aggression factors; LA = long-term pro-aggression factors.)

major classes of pro-aggression factors, so too are there two types of anti-aggression factor: long-term and situational. Long-term anti-aggression factors are more or less internalized and integrated features of an individual's personality system, and include values, norms, attitudes, and moral codes which dictate against aggression.

LONG-TERM NONAGGRESSION FACTORS

Obviously the most basic personality characteristic which could be associated with nonviolence is the individual's failure to learn any aggressive behaviors in the first place. If people do not have a basic repertoire of aggressive acts which they can use, they obviously cannot behave aggressively in even the most extreme of circumstances. As we have seen, however, nearly everyone is exposed to other people who are aggressive in at least limited respects, and so it would be the rare person indeed who had not acquired at least basic aggressive responses. Therefore, in the discussions which follow it will be assumed that individuals have learned some aggressive behaviors and that, given some provocation, they are at least potentially capable of violence. The question then becomes, what factors serve to prevent aggression when some provocation is present.

The extent to which individuals learn aggression will help determine whether provocation is met with violence or with some other response. It will also determine whether and to what extent people are capable of being provoked. Those who are exposed to a variety of aggressive models will undoubtedly acquire more extensive aggressive repertoires than people who are rarely exposed to others' aggression. Those who live in a violent subculture are apt to be exposed to many aggressive models, and they are most likely to act violently upon (and often with only slight) provocation. On the other hand, people who rarely observe aggression in others are unlikely to think of acting aggressively in any but the most extreme circumstances.

For any given individual, provocation may lead to aggression or to a number of nonaggressive responses, depending upon the strength of the provocation and the relative weighting of pro- and anti-aggression factors in the situation. For those who have in the past been rewarded for aggression, who have developed few inhibitions against aggression, and who have learned an extensive repertoire of aggressive behaviors, aggression will be a highly probable response. For those who have had little experience with aggression and have not been extensively exposed to aggressive models, aggression will be a fairly improbable response. Aggression becomes less probable when individuals are able to tolerate provocations well and are able to examine the situation from the other person's point of view. The different degrees of tolerance for frustration, anger, and fear which people acquire enable them to withstand different degrees of unpleasant emotional states before becoming physically assaultive. Furthermore, if an individual has learned a large number of alternative responses to provocation, aggression being only one of these, he is more apt to use some nonaggressive response. In other words, the more alternative behaviors an individual can engage in, the less the probability that he will respond aggressively. There are

a number of reasons why this may be so. First, if an individual
must choose one behavior from many possibilities, he must stop
and decide which behavior to select. This process involves time,
reflection, and cognitive activity, and therefore minimizes the
chances of acting impulsively. Second, even if the person chooses
a behavioral response at random, the more nonaggressive alternatives he has available, the less likely his choice will involve
aggression.

The Evaluation of Behavior

Not only are behavior patterns and basic repertoires learned at
an early age, but people also learn to evaluate and attach labels
to the behaviors they observe and learn. The evaluation of aggressive behaviors—either their own or that of others—depends
on who is doing the aggressing, against whom, and for what purpose. Few people consider aggression ipso facto good and few
consider it wholly worthless. If the aggressor is one with whom
the individual closely identifies and the victim of aggression one
whom he or she dislikes, then the aggression will be seen as more
justifiable and its magnitude as less severe than if the roles of aggressor and victim were reversed.[2] Students and student sympa-
thizers, for example, do not usually regard the student occupa-
tion of a university administration building as a violent act,
while nonstudents and nonsympathizers do. Attitudes and values also influence the choice of people with whom one identifies
and determines what actions are labeled violent. This can be
seen clearly in the case of terrorists. In November 1973, Arab
guerillas killed thirty-one people in Rome during an attack on a
United States airplane and took hostages on another plane to
Athens and eventually to Kuwait. When they gave themselves
up, they flashed victory signs, and one of the guerillas said: "We
are Palestinian Arabs, proud of what we did. . . . We are not
criminals. The criminals are those who bomb Palestinian refugee
camps in Lebanon."[3] By implication, the more people with
whom one identifies, the less justified would be aggression di-

rected against them (but the more justifiable it would be for them to aggress).

Evaluative labels attached to actions, people, and situations may be acquired through either classical or operant conditioning or a combination of both (see Chapter 2). Children may hear aggression discussed negatively by parents, teachers, or peers and thereby come to regard it negatively themselves. Operant conditioning of negative evaluations of aggression may thus occur if the child fails to be rewarded or praised for his or her aggression. As we have seen earlier, most children do observe at least some others behaving aggressively and receiving rewards of one sort or another as a consequence. At the same time, some of the child's own aggressive behavior may be punished, either directly by parents or indirectly because it failed to bring about the child's intended consequences. The product of this inconsistency of reward and punishment is likely to be evaluative ambiguity about the usefulness and appropriateness of aggression. The child will be uncertain as to whether aggression is good or bad, useful or not. Inconsistencies of reward and punishment for aggression and the resulting emotional uncertainty as to its usefulness may make a person hesitant about aggressing and will, in many cases, result in feelings of guilt or anxiety once aggression has been performed. In addition, the timing of rewards and punishments has been shown to be important in determining the extent of learning. If aggression is punished after a considerable delay (or if it is rewarded immediately), subsequent nonaggressive behavior will be weaker than if the punishment was immediate (or if the reward was delayed).[4]

The potency of rewards and punishments for learning to inhibit aggression can be seen in the striking sex differences in violent behavior. Males of all ages are more violent than females of comparable ages, and they are arrested for more crimes (with the exception of vice and prostitution) than females.[5] These differences are at least in part because of early training.[6] It would be expected, as the socialization of girls changes to become more comparable to the socialization of boys, that the difference between male and female violence would diminish. That is, if parents begin to rear their daughters in a way that they previously reserved for their sons, then girls would be encouraged to be assertive and would be less often punished for aggressive behavior and less often rewarded for passivity. In such situations we could expect increases in the rates of aggression for females. Evidence for this as seen in the decrease in the rates of violent crime between males and females has already been noted.[7]

In a nationwide survey of American men conducted in 1969 by Blumenthal and her colleagues[8] at the University of Michigan, it was found that only about 6 per cent of the men regarded all types of violence unfavorably and 3 per cent regarded all types of violence favorably. The remaining 91 per cent had no unequivocal good or bad label for violence, but instead judged specific acts of violence as good or bad depending upon who was aggressing against whom. Values toward others and their relationship to attitudes toward violence were also studied in the survey. Five types of values were examined: the extent to which an individual believed in retribution; kindness, as embodied in the Golden Rule; the right to self-defense; how people were valued relative to property; and how humanistic values were regarded in comparison to materialistic values.

Retributiveness and self-defense were most closely related to . . . attitudes (toward violence), while kindness was almost totally unrelated. Not only were the two "pro-violent" values (retributiveness and self-defense) closely related to attitudes about how much force the police should use in the control of disturbances, but there was a high degree of agreement with such values among American men. So it would seem that there are strong values in our country favoring violence for social control, and only weak values that act against it. . . . The value of kindness, which showed little or no effect among whites, was influential among blacks. The more a black man expressed a belief in kindness, the less likely he was to advocate violence. . . . In summary then, values are related to attitudes toward violence and probably influence such attitudes.

Since the vast majority of people regard violence as neither fully desirable nor fully undesirable, it will be necessary to examine peoples' own internal standards for deciding which behaviors are right or wrong and in which circumstances.

Internal Moral Restraints Against Violence

There are at least four kinds of justification which can play a role in an individual's failure to engage in violent behavior. The first is because he has no reason, desire, or ability to do so; the second is that, even though he may be motivated to aggress, he fails to act violently for fear of punishment, retaliation, or some other force acting upon him from the external environment; the third is that, even though motivated to aggress, an individual has available to him a variety of nonaggressive, alternative behaviors which enable him to cope with the provocation nonviolently; and finally, even though motivated to aggress, an individual may decide *for reasons he provides himself* that it is wrong, immoral, or unjust. In the last two cases, the individual decides not to aggress because of internal, rather than external, sources of pressure.

The development of internal moral restraint is a complex and much-debated issue in contemporary psychology. There are few definitive studies in this field, and much of what is presented below is based on current theories of moral development. What is generally meant by morality is behavior which is internally or self-regulated; behavior which is judged by the individual against some internal standard of right or wrong. It is possible that one's internalized standards are not seen as "moral" by the community at large. We can imagine a person, for example, raised and socialized by criminals who internalizes criminal values, behaviors, and standards. What is characteristic of an internal standard is that it is not dependent on the sentiments of others once it has developed.

Martin Hoffman[9] has indicated three types or levels of behavioral standard. The simplest and most primitive type involves fear or anxiety. Someone other than the actor must be present and be potentially capable of rewarding or punishing the actor's behavior. In the case of aggression, a person operating at this type of moral level would fail to engage in violence if some powerful authority figure were present, such as a parent or a policeman. The individual will not engage in an act because he has been punished for it in the past and may anticipate receiving punishment for engaging in the same act in the future. In the absence of a potentially rewarding or punishing person, there is no reason why the individual should *not* act aggressively. This is not an internal standard, but is based on potential forces from the external environment acting upon the individual. A second type of standard involves the individual's identification with some other person. The individual's actions are based on his views of what the other would approve or disapprove; his behavior is largely designed to be consistent with, and meet the approval of, the other. The person will not act aggressively so long as the individual with whom he identifies is perceived as condemning aggression. In the most advanced type of standard, the individual chooses his actions to meet his own obligations to himself. The individual does not require either the real or symbolic presence of another; he does not agress because he does not choose to agress.

How an individual progresses from one behavioral standard to another is a source of debate in psychology. Some have argued that the development of a higher level of moral behavior can be explained wholly or primarily by traditional theories of learning and conditioning,[10] while others, most notably Jean Piaget and Lawrence Kohlberg,[11] have stated that the transition from one level of morality to another is largely because of biological and cognitive maturation. While the processes involved in moral development are highly controversial at the moment, there is general acceptance of the existence of several levels of moral reasoning which people typically display. There are, however, some disagreements between theorists as to what are the levels of morality. Piaget, for example, distinguishes between two major moral levels: behavior regulated by a respect for, and submission to, authority and behavior which is self-regulated. In the former case, an individual obeys rules and laws *because* they are rules and laws which are seen as absolute and immutable. At such a level of moral judgment, the rightness or wrongness of an act is judged on the basis of its consequences; the more damaging an act, the worse it is seen to be, whether it was intentional or accidental. At the higher level of morality, rules and laws are seen as based on cooperative social arrangement and as subject to change. When judging whether an act is right or wrong, the person considers the intentions of the actor rather than simply the consequences of the act. At this level an intentional but slightly damaging act would be seen as more severe than an accidental act with extreme damage resulting.

Kohlberg has refined Piaget's levels of morality to include essentially a six-stage hierarchy. The first stage of moral reasoning involves, as does Piaget's, the avoidance of punishment and deference to authority. At the sixth or highest stage, an individual's behavior is governed by his or her own conscience and by mutual respect and trust.*

Important for the transition from one moral level to another is the ability to put oneself in the position of another person, to be able to view behavior from more than a self-interested perspective. When one is able to consider another's point of view, one is more likely to consider the other's intentions and feelings. This in turn is likely to result both in greater feelings of sympathy and empathy toward others and in a thought process involving reflection and evaluation which minimizes the tendency toward impulsive action.[12] Thus, higher levels of moral judgment are negatively related to aggressiveness.[13] In other words, the

---

* According to Kohlberg, differences between children of different social classes are due, not to a difference in values and moral precepts, but to the fact that they progress through the various stages of the hierarchy at different rates.

ability to step outside oneself and view a situation from the viewpoint of another increases one's self-control or cognitive control over one's own behavior and increases the number of behavioral options one has available. It has also been proposed that conflicts between parties can be reduced more readily by making each party state the views of the opposition accurately before discussing those views.[14] Thus taking another's perspective can not only serve to reduce conflict already present, but a tendency to take another's viewpoint can prevent conflict from arising in the first place.

A related factor of importance, which is also compatible with the earlier discussion of impulsivity and delay of gratification in Chapter 2, has been pointed out by Eleanor Maccoby[15] of Stanford University:

> One aspect of cognitive growth which might be related to moral behavior is increasing time span. The young child can neither plan over an extended time nor easily foresee delayed consequences of his actions. Increasing understanding of time sequences should facilitate moral behavior in that it permits more sophisticated understanding of the consequences of actions for oneself and others and permits balancing alternative outcomes in such a way that the individual can forego immediate gratifications for the sake of maximizing long-term gains and minimizing long-term losses.

At higher levels of moral reasoning, then, people are less impulsive and more reflective in their actions, are better able to foresee the consequences of their behavior, are more likely to consider the point of view of the other, and have available to themselves, as a consequence, a greater variety of alternative behaviors in which to engage. Closely related to the increase in behavioral alternatives which results from moral development is the intentional fostering of alternative forms of behavior, such as charity and altruism, which can serve as substitute responses to aggression in interpersonal situations.

At the higher levels of moral development, it is easier to sympathize with others and such sympathetic emotional responses are generally incompatible with feelings of rage and hostility. We would therefore expect those operating at the higher levels of moral reasoning to engage in behaviors opposite to and incompatible with aggression. To someone operating at an elementary moral level, the sight of a weakling or a drunk on the street may be an invitation to rob or attack, while to someone operating at a higher level of moral judgment, the sight of the same person is apt to elicit positive emotional responses.* To the extent that positive emotional responses are present, aggressive behavior becomes less probable.

Level of moral reasoning is related to a wide variety of behavioral and emotional tendencies. In a number of studies, support has been provided for the notion that higher levels of moral judgment are associated with increased positive social behavior and with decreased antisocial actions. For example, Fishkin, Keniston, and MacKinnon[17] found the higher levels of Kohlberg's moral reasoning stages to be associated with a rejection of conservative ideology (though it was not related to an acceptance of radical ideology). Individuals at the higher levels of moral reasoning are less likely to engage in cheating than those at lower levels.[18] An interesting study by Hudgins and Prentice[19] compared the level of moral judgment of delinquent and nondelinquent boys and of their mothers. They report that delinquents operated at lower levels of moral reasoning than nondelinquents, and further, that the mothers of delinquents also operated at lower moral judgment levels than the mothers of nondelinquents.

One correlate of increased moral judgment is an increase in the number of alternative behaviors from which an individual can choose in responding to some provocation or threat. Among the most important alternative behaviors are those which are incompatible with aggression, such as charity and altruism.

---

* This stands somewhat in contrast to Lerner's notion of the "just world phenomenon" presented in the previous chapter. Berkowitz, however, has provided evidence that the just world phenomenon is more likely to be found among those who are uncertain of their own self-worth.[16]

The Development of Responses Incompatible with Aggression

In any given situation, an individual can respond with either positive, neutral, or negative emotions and behaviors. To the extent that positive emotions and responses predominate, negative ones become less probable. A positive behavior is used here in the sense of adding something of value, either real or psychological, to another person, while a negative behavior is something which diminishes some real or psychological resource of another.[20] Generally, negative behavior is physically or psychologically injurious to another, while positive behavior is rewarding or pleasurable to another.

For young children, positive forms of social behavior are correlated with aggression. A young child who is aggressive toward another child is also likely to act kindly toward him or her at some other time. Beyond the age of about six, however, those children who are charitable and helpful toward others show the least amount of aggressive behavior.[21] For older children, and for adults as well, prosocial responses are negatively correlated with aggression, and to the extent that an individual has learned prosocial behaviors, he or she is not likely to be aggressive.[22] One reason for this relationship is the emotional requirements for prosocial forms of behavior. In order to be charitable and helpful toward others, one must be able to place oneself in the other's position, to see things from the other's point of view. This ability increases sympathy and empathy, making charitableness more likely and negative, incompatible forms of behavior, less likely.

The numerous studies of prosocial behavior have been adequately reviewed in the volumes edited by Macaulay and Berkowitz and Wispé.[23] Of central concern here is how such behaviors develop and how they are maintained over time. Wispé[24] presents definitions of various forms of positive social behavior, such as helping, which involves giving time and effort to another or another's cause, charity, which involves material sacrifice, and emergency intervention, which requires not only time and effort, but also involves personal involvement and often personal danger. We will use the general terms prosocial behavior, positive social behavior, and anti-aggression to include all of these.

What tends to make one act prosocially? Hornstein[25] has suggested three conditions which promote positive social behavior, all involving an increased feeling of commonality with others: aging, the lack of alienation, and a large inclusive concept of "we." According to Hornstein's formulation, the more people with whom one feels bonds of community, the more sympathy one feels toward them, and the more apt one is to act prosocially toward them. Aging has the effect of increasing the number of different social groups to which an individual belongs, and as the number of groups with which a person identifies increases, the number of people toward whom the person feels amity increases. Feelings of alienation tend to make the individual feel relatively isolated and powerless and reduce the number of others with whom the person feels common bonds. The obverse of this state, what Stanford University psychologist P. G. Zimbardo and others[26] have called "deindividuation," tends to increase feelings of involvement and participation in the social community. Finally, the distinction between one's concept of "we" and "they" is important in determining prosocial behavior. If an individual has an inclusive, broad concept of "we," for example, all mankind, he will have positive sentiments toward others in general. If other people are seen as somehow different, as belonging primarily to groups with which the individual does not identify in any way, there is less reason to sympathize with them and less charity will be extended toward them.

Ervin Staub, a psychologist at the University of Massachusetts, has suggested a number of additional determinants of prosocial behavior, among the most important of which is the general quality of interaction which occurs between parent and child.[27] To the degree that parents are affectionate and nurturant and to the extent that they use this affection and nurturance to guide and control the child's behavior, the child will develop positive regard for others and an internalized code of moral conduct. In addition, reasoning with the child, pointing out the consequences of his or her actions for others (a process known as induction), also serves to increase the child's ability to delay self-interested, egoistic behavior and to consider others' feelings before acting.

In general, affectionate, nurturant, inductive parents serve as models of morality to the child. As we have seen, when children are exposed to models who perform specific actions in the absence of punishment, observers will learn and imitate similar kinds of responses. So children for whom one or both parents serve as moral models are apt to imitate and eventually to internalize their parents' moral standards.

This fact is particularly evident in a study conducted by Perry London and his colleagues.[28] Twenty-seven Christians who rescued Jews from the Nazis in Europe were interviewed in depth about the reasons for their selfless acts. An important finding of the study was that nearly all of the rescuers identified strongly with one of their parents, who served as a highly moral model to their children. An additional finding of the study was that not all of the rescuers acted out of feelings of compassion. London describes one rescuer, a Seventh Day Adventist minister:

> Seventh Day Adventists were very marginal socially and not always treated kindly in Holland; his father spent considerable time in jail. Although this minister described himself as mildly anti-Semitic, like his father, during the war he organized a very effective and large-scale operation for rescuing Dutch Jews. The reason he gave for doing so was simply that it was a Christian's duty.

SITUATIONAL NONAGGRESSION FACTORS

Most theorists of moral development regard behavior which is under one's own regulation, that is behavior judged by internal standards, as somehow "more moral" than behavior which is guided by external standards, such as rules or laws. I have suggested that the reason for this is because external regulation requires the presence—either real or symbolic—of some potentially rewarding or punishing agent, while self-regulated behavior does not. Also, internally regulated behavior is likely to be more consistent across times and situations, while externally regulated behavior will be more unstable, varying with the circumstances and the particular others present. While it may be the case that internal regulation is more desirable from the viewpoint of society than external regulation, it is nevertheless true that much behavior depends on the specific circumstances in which the actor finds himself. In this section we will consider situation-specific behaviors.

Situational determinants of aggression were presented in Chapter 3 where it was proposed that situations account for at least as much aggressive behavior as the aggressor's personality, early developmental, and social history. This also seems to be the case with nonaggressive behavior, particularly prosocial responses. While the ideal may be that individuals internalize strong codes of moral conduct, develop broad and inclusive feelings of mutuality with others, place themselves in others' positions before deciding which course of action to follow, and follow their conscience rather than social convention, such an ideal is only rarely realized. The reason for this is because of the inconsistency and complexity of moral (and legal) codes of conduct as well as the competing and contradictory features of any given social situation. For example, while it may be seen as immoral to take another's life, it seems both legally and morally justifiable to do so if that other person threatens to take your own life. The difficulty of interpreting "correct" actions in complex situations can be seen in the case of the My Lai massacre. In nationwide surveys conducted in the United States and Australia[29] assessing reactions to the massacre and to the trial of Lt. William Calley, it was found that over half the Americans and nearly one-third of the Australians said that if ordered to shoot civilians, they would follow orders. Thus, there is both a good deal of uncertainty as to which course of action is proper and, for many respondents, some conflict between internal moral codes and external legal codes. Situations are rarely unambiguous, and so it becomes necessary to examine the components of situations which give rise to various kinds of definitions and behaviors.

If people generally or frequently fail to operate at the ideal level of morality, what situational factors prevent them from wrong-doing and promote acts of a positive social nature? One is the fear of punishment. Children often refrain from aggressive and other antisocial acts when their parents (or other adults) are present, but engage in them freely when adults are absent from the setting. Adults, too, will frequently resist the temptation to transgress when their behavior is, or may be, under surveillance.* Probably more important than the fear of direct punishment from others is self-elicited anxiety or guilt which may be aroused by a moral transgression. If, in the past, an individual has been punished or chastised for engaging in some behavior, say, aggression, he may refrain from aggressing even in the absence of others because he may anticipate some punishment (even though there is no one available to punish him) should he aggress. Such anticipation of punishment is roughly equivalent to the concept of anxiety; it is an unpleasant emotional state which is objectively unwarranted by the situation. This anticipation of punishment, or anxiety, may be prevented by not engaging in the aggressive act, thereby avoiding the feeling, or, if aggression has already occurred, anxiety may be reduced by self-punishment or self-criticism or by seeking punishment from others.[31] Each year many people report themselves to the police for crimes which they did not commit. One explanation for this phenomenon is that they are seeking punishment for some transgression which they did commit but for which they failed to receive the anticipated punishment.[32] Since this kind of aggression anxiety is an unpleasant state, we would

* An experiment conducted by the police department in Kansas City, Missouri, indicates that surveillance in the form of police car patrols may have little effect on the crime rate. Whether foot patrols influence the rate of crime is presently unknown.[30]

expect people to try to avoid its occurrence; one way to prevent such anxiety from arising is to avoid engaging in aggressive behavior.

It has been proposed that feelings of alienation tend to reduce prosocial behavior while feelings of individuation tend to increase it. We would thus expect people who live in small towns, as opposed to large cities, to be both more altruistic and less aggressive because of their feelings of integration and visibility in the community; findings which confirm this have been reported in a number of studies.[33]

Newman[34] suggests that the ability to be seen by others in multi-dwelling housing units acts as a powerful deterrent to crime.

> . . . We find that there are many aspects and facets to surveillance which contribute to the improvement of security. Stated simply, if there is any modicum of morality and accompanying social pressures in a community, opening up all activity in public spaces to natural supervision proves a very powerful deterrent to criminal acts. . . . The subdivision of housing projects into small, recognizable and comprehensible-at-a-glance enclaves is a further contributant to improving the visual surveillance mechanism. Simultaneously, this subdivision serves to provide identity and territorial definition; gives focus, involvement, and commitment to the act of surveillance. In some housing developments, where the surveillance of the activity of one's neighbors, outside their apartments, was possible, residents were found to be very familiar indeed with everyone's comings and goings—and occasionally, somewhat critical. The overall effect, however, was to cement collective identity and responsibility—through these social pressures.

It is of interest here to note the psychological effects which physical structures may have and the resultant influence of these various psychological states. In the examples cited by Newman, particular types of dwelling units enhance feelings of community and identity among residents and, by making any intruder easily identifiable, minimize crime.

Table 4.1

Factors associated with aggression and nonaggression

	Short-term	Long-term
Aggression	*Characteristics of the actor:* Immediately prior aggressive acts. Loss of cognitive control of behavior. Low identifiability. Moderate amount of alcohol ingestion. Moderate emotional arousal. *Consequences of actor's behavior:* Cognitive justification for aggression. Devaluation of victim. *Environmental factors:* Abundant opportunities for aggression. Availability of a weapon. Familiar environment. Familiar or similar target. Recent exposure to violence.	*Characteristics of the actor:* Deindividuation. Impulsivity. Low level of moral judgment. Negative labels for targets. Positive labels for aggression. *Consequences of actor's behavior:* Rewards for aggression. *Parental characteristics:* Aggressive models, unpunished. High punitiveness. *Environmental factors:* Aggressible situations. Exposure to aggression in others.

	Short-term	Long-term
Nonaggression	*Characteristics of the actor:* Aggression anxiety, guilt. Arousal of pleasant emotions. Fear of punishment. High identifiability. Immediately prior nonaggressive acts. *Environmental factors:* Presence of authority figure (for those low in moral judgment). Unfamiliar environment.	*Characteristics of the actor:* Ability to delay gratification. Ability to take role of others. High level of moral judgment. Inclusive concept of "we." Individuation. Negative labels for aggression. Positive regard for others. *Consequences of actor's behavior:* Rewards for nonaggression. *Parental characteristics:* Affection, control, nurturance. Nonaggressive models. *Environmental factors:* Nonaggressible situations.

Note: The characteristics of the actor listed under short-term factors are temporary or transient states, most often induced by the physical or social environment, rather than enduring traits of the actor.

Not only does the physical environment influence feelings of identity and behavior, but it can also influence the creation of a wide variety of mood states and opportunities for engaging in various acts. Individuals' immediate moods, experiences, and opportunities may influence their prosocial as well as their antisocial tendencies. For example, during the Christmas season opportunities to engage in prosocial behavior are abundant: there are Salvation Army kettles on street corners and in shopping centers, mail order campaigns for Christmas seals, drives to raise funds, and clothing, food, and toy collections for the needy. The increased number of opportunities for helping are likely to have an "unfreezing" effect on charitable motives; and either by observing the charity of others, who serve as altruistic models,[35] or by experiencing the generally positive emotions which accompany a holiday season,[36] individuals are more likely to engage in prosocial behavior themselves. Positive opportunities and emotional states facilitate prosocial behavior and impede aggressive behavior.

In the same way that a single act of aggression may promote subsequent aggressive acts, so too may a single act of charity facilitate subsequent altruistic acts by the same person. For example, Freedman and Fraser[37] made a simple, small request of people and later made a larger request of them. Those who complied with the first request were more likely to comply with the second. By the same token, once one has engaged in prosocial behavior, there may be an increased tendency to continue to act positively toward others.

The aggression model used throughout this book may be modified slightly to account for this effect and to generate expectations about other aspects of altruistic behavior. Once there is some incentive to engage in prosocial behavior (for example, hearing a cry for help), an individual will evaluate the situation in order to determine whether that prosocial incentive is stronger than the competing elements in the setting which call for a nonhelping response (for example, the potential danger involved, the loss of time and energy). If the prohelping factors are seen to outweigh the nonhelping factors, then the individual will offer assistance. Once such action has occurred, the individual will justify his or her behavior by re-evaluating the situation and the other people involved. It is this re-evaluation, which amounts to a cognitive justification for helping, which facilitates helping on subsequent occasions. In the study reported in Chapter 3 by Goldstein, Davis, and Herman, once an individual acted prosocially toward another he or she subsequently engaged in greater and greater amounts of prosocial behavior as the experiment progressed.

There is generally a conflict involved in helping another person either because of the costs of time, energy, money, and potential danger involved or the cultural norms which stress minding one's own business. This conflict is resolved in much the same way that aggression conflict is resolved: the individual attempts to make sense out of the situation by weighing each of the component elements of the situation. When the prohelping factors are seen to outweigh the nonhelping factors, help will ensue. The weighting of the people, settings, and behaviors involved depends both on long-term factors, such as exposure to helping models and rewards for helping in the past, and on situational factors, such as the estimated costs and rewards for helping in that particular situation. As with aggression, once a helping act has occurred, it will tend to be justified in the individual's mind by re-evaluating more positively the prohelping elements and devaluing the nonhelping elements.

Before going on to discuss the control of violence, it might serve us well to summarize the contributing factors to aggression which have been presented so far. Table 4.1 contains a listing of the causative aggression and nonaggression factors reviewed in Chapters 2 through 4.

REDUCTION AND CONTROL OF VIOLENCE

5

For we have at hand great quantities of research findings which clearly indicate what we should be doing. Much indeed we don't know, but we are not doing one-tenth of what we should about what we already do know.

Karl Menninger[1]

There are two major ways in which violence and aggression can be controlled. The first, a short-term measure, is to prevent people already capable of and motivated to engage in violence from expressing their aggressive desires; the second, a long-term goal, is to prevent the ability and desire to aggress from arising in the first place. The present chapter concerns the reduction of violence among people who have already been socialized in aggression to a greater or lesser degree.

The model of aggression which has been used to this point suggests that aggressive behavior is the result of four factors: long-term and situational factors positively associated with aggression and long-term and situational factors negatively associated with aggression. The likelihood of aggressive behavior is a result of the ratio of these two sets of opposing tendencies. The model further implies that aggression can be lessened in at least four ways: by reducing long-term pro-aggression factors, by reducing situational pro-aggression factors, by increasing long-term nonaggression factors, and by increasing situational nonaggression factors. Long-term factors, characterized as internalized aspects of an individual's personality which arise during socialization, will be discussed in the following chapter. Situational factors, characterized as more or less ephemeral, short-lived, and external to the individual's personality, will be discussed below.

Before proceeding to discuss ways to control violence, some mention of the implementation of these controls should be made. While the problem of violence may be primarily psychological, as I would argue (after all, violence involves the interaction of two or more individuals, and this is the primary concern of social psychology), the problem is not *merely* psychological. Rather, any such problem has a political, a social, a psychological, and an economic component, and so one can look at the causes or effects of violence and crime in political, economic, social, or psychological terms. For example, Henry and Short[2] examined the economic correlates of homicide and suicide; Feierabend and Feierabend[3] have explored the economic and political conditions conducive to violence; and numerous sociologists and criminologists[4] have portrayed violence as the result of social factors of one type or another.

The National Commission on the Causes and Prevention of Violence recognized the complexity of the problem when it stated:

> For remedial social change to be an effective moderator of violence, the changes must command a wide measure of support throughout the community. Official efforts to impose change that is resisted by a dominant majority frequently prompts counter-violence.

And Erich Fromm[5] has more recently argued:

. . . in order to reduce group narcissism, the misery, monot-
ony, dullness, and powerlessness that exist in large sectors of
the population would have to be eliminated. This cannot be
accomplished simply by bettering material conditions. It can
only be the result of drastic changes in the social organization
to convert it from a control-property-power orientation to a
life orientation; from *having* and *hoarding* to *being* and *sharing*.
It will require the highest degree of active participation and
responsibility on the part of each person in his role as a worker
or employee in any kind of enterprise, as well as in his role as
a citizen. Entirely new forms of decentralization must be de-
vised, as well as new social and political structures that will
put an end to the society of anomie, the mass society consisting
of millions of atoms.

Thus, despite political and economic efforts to control violence, without social support such efforts are bound to fail. It
will therefore be necessary to go beyond the psychological causes
of violence discussed earlier. While the solutions to violence are
seen as primarily psychological—that is, as requiring changes in
the learning of behavior, values, norms, and so on—it will be
necessary to implement them politically and to develop widespread social and economic support for them.

Since psychology (or any other branch of science) does not
have sufficient justification for suggesting any future course of
action, it will be necessary to go beyond existing theory and
data in order to suggest remedies. While much of what follows
is consistent with scientific literature, it is not possible for me to
know the extent to which my personal, idiosyncratic beliefs have
colored my proposals. Therefore, rather than dictating solutions
to aggression and crime, I much prefer to think of the proposals
below as hypothetical statements which need to be tested on a
small scale before they are adopted as policy. While some of the
solutions discussed below are likely to work and others are not,
what is most important is that *implemented solutions to social
problems not contradict what we do know about those problems
from a scientific standpoint.* (This implies that in at least some

cases proposed solutions will contradict traditional folk wisdom about social problems; but "common sense" has not fared too well in solving complex human problems in the last two or three thousand years.)

One further point needs to be made about proposed solutions to social problems, and this concerns the ethical and moral nature of acceptable remedies. For example, it is now possible to perform surgery directly on the brain in order to remove or sever those brain centers believed to be involved in aggressive behavior, a procedure commonly known as *psychosurgery*. In many instances, psychosurgery seems to decrease violence significantly. (In many instances it decreases other, unrelated behaviors as well. In fact, psychosurgery does not differ greatly from the first primitive attempts to regulate criminal behavior. The penalty for stealing in the ancient Code of Hammurabi was removal of the offender's hands; modern surgical techniques would leave the hands intact but prevent the offender from using them.) The question has been raised as to whether those on whom such surgery is performed are capable of giving their "informed consent" to the procedure, and the answer seems to be that, in general, they are not. So while psychosurgery may eliminate violence in some people, it is done essentially without their permission and often without their knowledge. Such a solution seems potentially worse than the problem it is designed to cure.[6] Furthermore, such remedies are essentially admissions of society's failure or unwillingness to deal with offenders in a humane and trusting fashion. Whatever solutions are adopted for dealing with violent and criminal behavior must respect the integrity (to say nothing of the Constitutional rights) of the offenders involved.*

Below we will consider a variety of solutions to aggression and

* While space does not permit discussion of the victims of violent crime, needless to say their freedoms and rights are to be equally protected. Among these protections, a program to compensate victims for injury and property loss should be instituted. Such a program would probably increase citizens' feelings of responsibility for others, and might thus serve as an indirect deterrent to crime.[7]

crime designed to curtail their prevalence immediately. Such measures, however, are remedial and should be implemented along with, and eventually be replaced by, the longer-term measures proposed in Chapter 6.

CHANGES IN THE PHYSICAL ENVIRONMENT AND CRIME CONTROL

If, as I have argued, most acts of violence are committed by not atypical people who are momentarily instigated to aggress and who have an appropriate target and means of aggressing, then the environment can be so altered as to minimize the means of aggressing, maximize cognitive or self-control over behavior, decrease the tendency for impulsive action, and heighten the actor's feelings of (or actual) identifiability. The environment, which can also provide varying opportunities for aggression, can be restructured to reduce the opportunity and "temptation" for antisocial behavior.

For example, research has been conducted on means to reduce the illegal use of slugs in parking meters. Decker[8] reports research in which certain structural features of parking meters were altered to minimize slug use. In New York City in 1970, over 3 per cent of all parking meter insertions were slugs. Had money been inserted instead of slugs, the total in additional revenues to the city would have been in the neighborhood of a half-million dollars. Two studies were conducted in an effort to determine the most effective means of reducing slug use. In one study, three different regions of the city were chosen, and in each region a different label was attached to each parking meter. The labels read:

Slug use is a violation of New York City Ordinance: $50 fine
Slug use is a violation of state law: 3 months imprisonment and $500 fine
Slug use is a federal crime: 1 year imprisonment and $1000 fine.

A fourth region was considered a control region and no labels were attached to the meters.

In a second study, Duncan VIP meters were installed in selected experimental regions. The Duncan parking meter rejects many types of slug and also displays the most recently inserted coin in a coin-view window. Thus, in the first study, variations in the potential punishment for slug use were introduced, while in the second study, physical characteristics of parking meters were altered.

Decker reports that the use of slugs declined in all of the areas in which labels were used, as well as in the control area in which no label was used. There were no significant differences in the rate of decline among the four areas studied. Hence, the use of the various warning labels was considered to have no effect since there was as much decline in slug usage in the no label (control) region as in the other three regions. However, in the areas in which the new Duncan meters were installed, declines in the rate of slug use were dramatic. Compared with the same areas before the installation of the new meters, slug usage declined from 26 per cent in one region to 80 per cent in another. Decker concludes:

> It is obvious that the parking meters with the coin-view window and slug-rejector device were more effective in reducing illicit slug use than use of warning labels. The minimal deterrent value of the labels can probably be attributed to the slim chance a slug user will be apprehended, much less convicted and subjected to the maximum penalty. This might indicate that potential slug users are not greatly deterred by the coin-view window either, since the object of the window is also to instill fear of apprehension. Hence, it seems that a mechanical device, such as the slug-rejector, which makes law violation difficult, is superior to a scheme or device which is dependent upon the potential violator's fear of apprehension. This finding is critical in light of the theoretical structure of criminology based on a punishment-deterrence-rehabilitation model, and it suggests a serious look at programs based on a prevention model and environmental design.

While the Decker report raises the interesting possibility that crime can be deterred by particular environmental features, the question arises as to whether more serious crimes can be so deterred. Although only limited research has been conducted on the effects of environmental modification, what little there is suggests that intelligent and well-planned changes in architectural and urban design can bring about a reduction of violent crime and theft.

Oscar Newman[9] discusses the case of Clason Point Gardens, a two-story public housing development in the Bronx, New York, consisting of four hundred duplex apartments located in over forty row-house buildings. Elderly white families comprise 33 per cent of the tenants, Puerto Rican families 25 per cent, and Negro families about 30 per cent. Newman states:

> Preliminary interviews revealed that tenants were extremely fearful of being victimized by criminals, both during the day and in the evening; they had severely changed or curtailed their patterns of activity as a result of the atmosphere of heightened danger; they felt they had no right to question, and were afraid to question, the presence of strangers as a means of anticipating and preventing crimes before they occurred. Adolescents from neighboring projects used the grounds as a congregation area, instilling fear and anger in many Clason Point residents.

Newman conducted interviews with the residents of the project in order to clarify what types of design changes were needed, and reasoned that increased tenant surveillance of the grounds, greater definition of the functions of the grounds, an increased sense of propriety by the residents, and a reduction of intergenerational conflict among residents were required. A variety of design changes were made in the project including the following:

> To highlight the public quality of the major pedestrian walk, the design called for (1) widening of the path, using colored and decoratively scored paving; (2) differentiating small pri-

vate areas (front lawns) outside each dwelling from the public path with low, symbolic walls; and (3) the addition of public seating in the center of the public path, located at a distance from private dwellings sufficient to eliminate conflicts over use, but close enough to be under constant surveillance by residents. At selected intersections of the primary and secondary paths, "play-nodes" were to be created for young children—with seating nearby to allow for supervision. New and decorative lighting was to be employed to highlight the new public paths and recreation areas at night, so as to extend the residents' surveillance potential and feelings of security.

In addition, buildings were refaced in a variety of colors selected by the tenants. The one area of Clason Point which residents felt was most dangerous was the central green space. This area was transformed into special use areas for young children, teenagers, and adults (see Figures 5.1 and 5.2). Newman hoped to turn the central area from a desolate one into the "new focus of Clason Point."

The results of the transformation of Clason Point are summarized by Newman:

> At this writing the rehabilitation of the project has been complete for over twelve months. During this test period, felonies were down to one-third of the previous year's level. Measures of tenant satisfaction showed statistically significant improvement in the reduction of fear, in increased surveillance on the part of tenants, and in their evaluation of the quality of their living environment. The newly modified central play area is very intensively used by the community, and this has succeeded in discouraging its use by drunks and addicts. Tenants now maintain some 80 percent of the project grounds, appreciably reducing the workload of the maintenance staff.

The psychological effects of various features of architectural design and spatial characteristics of the environment are only in the initial stages of exploration.[10] Nevertheless, it is known that conditions which increase the individual's sense of self, that

Figure 5.1. View of Central Square before modifications. The most dangerous area in Clason Point Gardens was identified both through tenant interviews and police reports as being the central square. This photo shows the square as it was, including a few benches and one pair of centrally located lights. Photo by O. Newman. Reprinted with permission.

is, conditions which maximize identifiability by others and the possibility of discovery and apprehension, will diminish the tendency to engage in antisocial acts. The design changes reported by Newman had the effects of increasing both the use of formerly unused areas and the visibility of open spaces. These in turn discouraged trespassers and loiterers and led to a reduction in the rate of crime, most probably by increasing would-be offenders' reflection on the consequences of such acts.

Newman also discusses the attempts of the upper- and middle-class urban resident to maximize safety by moving to high-rise

Figure 5.2. View of modified central area. The area has been transformed into a community recreation facility. It has been extensively lighted for night use. Photo by O. Newman. Reprinted with permission.

luxury apartments protected by electronic surveillance systems and round-the-clock doormen. Tenants are likely to have double-locked doors, a wide-angle viewer in entrance doors, and other security devices. While such measures of safety may add to the immediate security of the urban unpoor, they present dangers to the community on a larger scale.

When people begin to protect themselves as individuals and not as a community, the battle against crime is effectively lost. The indifferent crowd witnessing a violent crime is by now an American cliché. The move of middle- and upper-class populations into protective high-rises and other structures of isolation —as well guarded and as carefully differentiated from the surrounding human landscape as a military post—is just as clearly a retreat into indifference. The form of buildings and their arrangement can either discourage or encourage people to take an active part in policing while they go about their daily business. "Policing" is not intended to evoke a paranoid vision but refers to the oldest concept in the Western political tradition: the responsibility of each citizen to ensure the functioning of the *polis*.[11]

A particular danger of the middle- and upper-class enclave in the city is that it provides security by limiting access to the building. "This usually means walling off a two- to ten-acre housing complex from the surrounding neighborhood. By this action, thousands of feet of street are removed from all forms of social and visual contact. A natural mechanism providing safety to our streets has been sacrificed to insure the security of the residents of the walled-off complex."

There are alternatives to the high-rise enclaves in which mutual surveillance of the streets and the buildings would be achieved. By maximizing the use of glass in lobbies, corridors, and apartments and by increasing the number of entrances, the streets could be easily surveilled by the residents of the complex and the complex by those in the street. The building would thus be an integrated and integral part of the community rather than isolated from it.

Aside from arranging buildings in such a way as to increase surveillance by occupants and passersby, it is possible to minimize opportunities for crime by altering other characteristics of the environment. For example, nearly half the automobiles stolen each year—about 200,000—have had the keys left in them by their owners. Removing the keys reduces the opportunity (or makes it more difficult) to steal the car. In 1965, when Chevrolet eliminated the "off" position from the ignition system—which previously enabled one to start the car without a key—thefts of Chevrolets dropped 50 per cent from the previous year.[12]

While such environmental measures may reduce criminal activity, it is unclear whether their effects are long-lasting. When

American automobile manufacturers began to install devices which would lead to the use of seat belts, such as a noxious buzzer which could be terminated only by fastening one's seat belt, it was not long before motorists figured out ways to "fool" the safety device; many drivers left the belts permanently fastened behind them. Devices designed to prevent theft and burglary may lead to more ingenious methods among those who are determined to steal. Nevertheless, many crimes, particularly those committed by juveniles, are simply crimes of opportunity, and if opportunities are reduced, such as through increased street lighting and better door latches, crimes which otherwise would be committed will not be.

One measure which would save thousands of lives annually, and which may indirectly be linked with aggression, would be the installation of a device which would prevent cars from being started by a driver who is drunk. The device would consist of either a "breathalyzer" to determine the extent of alcohol in the driver's system or a reaction-time device which an inebriated driver could not operate satisfactorily.

THE DIFFERENCE BETWEEN AN ASSAULT AND A HOMICIDE IS A GUN

In Paris, whose metropolitan area includes 6.5 million people, there were 255 murders in 1970 and fewer than 1000 robberies. In Tokyo, where there were nearly eleven and one-half million people in 1970, there were 213 murders, 474 robberies, and 500 rapes. Among the more than 8 million people in London in 1970, there were 51 homicides and 7 rapes. In 1970, New York City's 7.9 million people committed 1,117 murders, 74,102 robberies, and 2,141 rapes.[13] These relative figures are not peculiar to the particular cities compared. Table 5.1 shows the relative figures for Baltimore, Maryland, and Liverpool, England. For the United States as a whole, the homicide rate (homicides per 100,000 population) is 34 times that of Denmark, 23 times that of Sweden, England, and Wales, 14 times that of Spain, 10

Aggression and Crimes of Violence

times that of Greece, and from 2 to nearly 70 times that of Australia, Austria, Canada, Finland, France, Hong Kong, Hungary, Ireland, Israel, Italy, Japan, Netherlands, New Zealand, Poland, Scotland, Switzerland, and West Germany.[14] One of the most perplexing problems facing any student of violence is why Americans seem so aggressive when compared to others with whom they appear to have so much in common.*

TABLE 5.1

A comparison of crime in Baltimore and Liverpool

	Baltimore	Liverpool
Population	918,000	745,750
Number of police	3,473	1,979
Murders	236	3
Rapes	675	0
Assaults	9,023	1,016
Robberies	8,864	466
Burglaries	19,367	15,586
Total number arrested	49,025	9,619

Figures are for the year 1969 and are adapted from the (London) *Daily Mirror,* July 9, 1970. Reprinted by permission of Syndication International Ltd.

A number of explanations have been offered for the disproportionate violence of the United States.[15] It has been argued that our history has been a violent one, that a nation born of revolution has a tradition of violence. It has also been proposed that the omnipresence of violence in the mass media is responsible for the high rate of interpersonal aggression reflected in our homicide statistics. Our particular brand of capitalism, in which competition in the economic sphere generalizes to result in competition in all areas of social conduct, has been seen as

* Before any conclusions are drawn from these figures alone, it should be pointed out that the different countries, and even localities within countries, have different procedures for defining and recording crime and that a number of countries do have higher homicide rates than the United States (for example, Ceylon, Colombia, Kuwait, Taiwan, and Venezuela).

the basis of violence in the society. The permissiveness of the society has also been held responsible, both with respect to our child-rearing practices and our system of jurisprudence—parents who are permissive with their children and courts which are lenient toward criminals have been seen as the cause of the violence in America. While there may be some justification for each of these claims, a more realistic picture incorporates all of them, as well as other features of American life. Of those countries with much lower violent crime rates than the United States, some were also born of revolution; some also have a relatively high incidence of violence in their media; some also are capitalistic; and some are even more lenient in child-rearing and toward criminals. One feature which may partially account for the differences in violent deaths is the relative unavailability of lethal weapons, particularly firearms, in most other industrialized nations. Because of the abundance of firearms in the United States, the opportunity to commit homicide is considerably greater than in most other countries.

Since the turn of the century, over three-quarters of a million citizens have been killed by gunfire in the United States. Each year, over 20,000 Americans are shot to death and over 200,000 are seriously injured by firearms. There is nearly one rifle, shotgun, or handgun for every two citizens of this country. In Britain, there are less than one million licensed rifles, handguns, and shotguns among all its 55 million inhabitants.

While there is some evidence that the mere possession or presence of a lethal weapon leads to increased violence, this evidence is in dispute (see Chapter 3, Ref. 50); and so a more conservative statement would be that, when an individual is bent on aggression in the first place, the presence of a weapon will eventuate in its use, and the consequence of the aggressive act will be much more severe than if no weapon were available. An angry husband may yell at his wife and may even hit her; if a knife is handy, he is more likely to stab her, and there is about a one in thirty chance that she will die of the stabbing. If a gun is handy, she is likely to be shot and will die in close to one-sixth of such shooting incidents. The nearly 100 million firearms in this country undoubtedly contribute to the American homicide rate, either directly by serving to provoke aggression or indirectly by enlarging the consequences and seriousness of aggression.

Morris and Hawkins[16] make several recommendations concerning gun control:

> All firearms—handguns, rifles, and shotguns—must be registered and all persons required to obtain a license to possess or carry any such weapon. . . . Other than in exceptional cases, a license to possess a handgun will be restricted to the police and to authorized security agencies. . . . Gun clubs, hunting clubs, and similar sporting associations using firearms will be required to store the firearms used by their members on club premises and to maintain close security over them.

However, such solutions to this problem are made complex largely because of opposition expressed by a number of individuals and groups with vested interests in maintaining the current system of manufacture and distribution of lethal weapons.

Morris and Hawkins go on to consider the traditionally posed objections to their gun control proposals. They refute the notion that, if guns were not available, murderers would simply use other weapons. Guns are more fatal than other weapons and therefore cause more deaths. It is also argued by some that when guns are outlawed only outlaws will have guns; but *murderers are relatively average people with no long history of previous violence; the availability of guns makes them murderers instead of simple assaulters*.

During the period when guns undergo registration and owners obtain licenses, it is recommended that all ammunition for firearms and all firearms themselves be made with radioactive tracer elements in them so that the presence of such weapons can be detected electronically. Morris and Hawkins further suggest that means for voluntary surrender of firearms without threat of penalty be provided and that the government offer to buy guns back at higher than traditional rates to minimize the temptation to sell guns on the black market. Such steps as restrictive licensing and the surrender of firearms will considerably diminish the rate of death due to homicide, suicide, and accident, but unless additional measures are provided for disarming the American people, there will still be a significant number of premature deaths in this country because of guns and rifles. Morris and Hawkins recommend severe penalties for weapons offenses and the banning of all sales of weapons through the mail. Such measures will indeed reduce the number of firearms in private hands, but a long-term goal is to make weapons unavailable to those who could use them lethally. It is proposed here that the manufacture of firearms be phased out and that their production ultimately be prohibited except under contract to an official agency of government. If citizens are disarmed sufficiently, then the often legitimate assumption of law enforcement officials that those suspected of crimes should be "considered armed and dangerous" will no longer be warranted, and the final step in disarmament will be a prohibition against carrying weapons by the police, along the lines of the British system, in which each police precinct has a few expert marksmen who are used only in situations in which the police are fired upon. Insofar as the Constitutional issue of disarmament is concerned, Morris and Hawkins state: "We are confident this [disarmament] offends no Constitutional sanctity; we do not oppose a militia whose right to bear arms is guaranteed by the Constitution."

CRIME AND TIME AND PUNISHMENT

One factor discussed as a situational determinant of nonaggression was the fear of punishment. It is most probable that once the fear of punishment is aroused in an individual, he is less likely to engage in aggressive behavior. The larger question concerns the circumstances under which the fear of punishment will be aroused. It is frequently suggested that penalties for various crimes, ranging from monetary fines to probation to imprisonment, serve as deterrents to crime by arousing the would-be criminal's fear or anxiety.

When violence occurs in the presence of others (or becomes known to others, as through the press) both the actor and the observer will show increased tendencies toward violence. These effects, as has been indicated, are curtailed when the aggressor receives immediate punishment for his aggression. In the case of criminal violence, punishment for aggression is usually delayed by lengthy legal proceedings, if indeed it is forthcoming at all. Hence, those who read about violence in their newspapers or see it on the news on television are essentially observers of unpunished aggressive models. Surveys of crime and subsequent legal proceedings indicate that only a minority of those suspected of engaging in criminal violence are apprehended.[17] (In fact, a sizable number of violent crimes go unreported to the police, particularly in cases of rape.) Of those who are apprehended for a crime, there is usually a considerable delay in bringing them to trial so that if punishment is delivered to the aggressor, it is delivered only long after the aggressive act has occurred. But in most cases of criminal violence punishment is either nominal or not delivered at all.

In a survey of the criminal justice system in Philadelphia,[18] it was found that prison sentences were relatively infrequent and that their length tended to be minimal (see Tables 5.2 and 5.3).

TABLE 5.2

Disposition of Philadelphia criminal cases

Outcome of all cases	Murder	Rape	Aggravated robbery	Aggravated assault and battery
Jail sentences	55%	23%	39%	16%
Probation	22	30	17	47
Charges dropped	12	29	29	20
Acquitted	11	18	15	17

Adapted from Barlett and Steele.

TABLE 5.3

Length of sentence by crime

	Murder	Rape	Aggravated robbery	Aggravated assault and battery
1 year or less	33%	55%	61%	75%
13 months to 5 years	47	42	32	25
more than 5 years	20	3	7	0

Note: The percentages above show the prison sentences imposed on those defendants who pleaded guilty or were found guilty. Adapted from Barlett and Steele.

About one-fifth of the defendants in cases of suspected crimes of violence were acquitted, about one-fourth had the charges against them dropped, and about one-third were placed on probation. Therefore, a total of only approximately one-fourth of those apprehended for acts of criminal violence were sentenced to prison. Campbell[19] reports that nationwide "only about half of the nine million serious crimes committed each year are reported to the police, only 12 per cent result in an arrest of a suspect, only 6 per cent result in a conviction, and only 1.5 per cent in the incarceration of the offender." Even if a much greater proportion were convicted and imprisoned, the long delay between the commission of a violent act and its punishment in a court of law may make whatever punishment is administered relatively ineffective, both to the aggressor and to observers in the community at large.

After being arrested for a violent crime, a defendant may be called before a judge and, if he is wealthy or lucky, be released on bail pending a hearing initiated by defense counsel or the actual trial of the case. Over 50 per cent of those arrested for serious personal crimes are released on bail, and the remainder are held in prison until their cases come to trial. In either event, the defendant is apt to be on good behavior between the time he is apprehended and the time his case comes to court since any further misconduct on his part is likely to increase the chances of receiving severe punishment. The period between arrest and disposition of a case often exceeds one year, during which time most defendants are able to lead noncriminal lives. The case, after this lengthy delay, now comes to trial and, assuming the defendant is found guilty and the judge is so disposed, the defendant is sentenced to some term in prison. Psychologically, what effects will this sequence of events have? First, we can ask what effects the punishment (prison sentence) is supposed to have, and second, what effects it will actually have.

Prison sentences are designed to serve several functions, although legal experts disagree on the relative importance of these: a *retributive* function, designed to punish the criminal for his misdeed; a *rehabilitative* function, designed to minimize the likelihood that the act will be repeated by the criminal in the future; a *deterrent or communicative* function, designed to serve warning to others that the act will be dealt with severely should they engage in it; a *protective* function, designed to segregate the criminal from the rest of society. One function often overlooked in such discussions is that criminal sentences are designed to make individuals accept *responsibility* for their actions.

According to one of the most well-established principles in psychology, the law of effect, we know that events closest in time to a punishment are more severely retarded by the punishment than events further removed from the punishment. In the typical case that we have described, an aggressive act occurs at $Time_1$ followed by nonaggressive acts at $Time_2$ followed by punishment at $Time_3$. According to the law of effect, behavior closest in time to the punishment will be more influenced by the punishment than behavior farther removed from it. Thus, the punishment is likely to have a greater effect on $Time_2$ behavior, the nonaggressive acts, than on $Time_1$ behavior, the aggressive act. (Of course, the defendant knows that the punishment is being administered to him because of his aggression and not because of the behavior intervening between that act and the punishment, and so the punishment will probably have at least some impact on the future likelihood of the particular aggressive act. Nevertheless, the longer the delay between the aggression and the punishment for it, the less effective the punishment in retarding aggressive behavior.) The typically long delay in our present system may severely retard whatever rehabilitative effect the punishment might otherwise have.

With respect to observers or those who learn of the crime and its subsequent punishment, we can ask what psychological principles might be invoked to explain the effects of punishment as a deterrent or communicative device. Given the long delay between a criminal act of violence and its subsequent disposition by the courts, two processes of importance arise. First is the probability that the act itself will be punished, rewarded, or neither. We saw in Chapter 2 that only when aggressive acts were punished was an observer unlikely to learn and imitate the aggressive behavior of the actor in appropriate circumstances. The Philadelphia survey indicated that in only about 25 per cent of the cases was a prison sentence imposed, and the Campbell paper reported the figure at about one-fifteenth of that. Hence, in the vast majority of cases an aggressive act occurs which observers see going unpunished.

In many of these cases, as well as in some of the instances in which punishment is imposed, the publicity given to the defendant may serve as a positive reinforcement to observers. That is, observers may perceive having one's name in the newspaper or mentioned on television as a reward, and this may increase the chances that observers will imitate the aggression. Former Attorney General Ramsey Clark[20] has noted:

> People otherwise docile for the time respond to reports of violence as if it were a contagious disease and the reports were a carrier. And for the kid from the slums the only time he is likely to see his picture in the paper may be when he is in police custody following arrest for a violent crime. Far from destroying a reputation, this is the best chance for fame—or at least notoriety—that fate offers him.

Since observers are apt to interpret some aspects of the situation as rewarding and since they observe punishment to the aggressor only in a relatively small proportion of the cases, we can see that the present system of jurisprudence can have only minimal impact as a deterrent. If this is unconvincing, add to it the period of months and often years which intervene between crime and punishment. Observers of an aggressive crime will probably dissociate the punishment from the crime after such a long period of time. Not only does the long delay minimize the effectiveness of punishment on the aggressor, it also minimizes its effectiveness as a communication to observers.[21]

One function of incarceration is to protect society from the criminal by removing him for a time from the community. Well over 90 per cent of all prisoners, however, are ultimately released from prison and usually within a matter of a few years. While in prison, the convict will associate with those who are often more versed in violence than himself, will be subjected to inhumane and degrading conditions and treatment, and will leave prison a much greater threat to society than when he first entered. Coupled with a "criminal" or "ex-convict" label for life, a former prisoner is often unable to find suitable employment, and, being considered a social deviant by those in the community, will most often have among his associates other social deviants. These are the very circumstances optimal for the commission of further illegal acts. So while imprisonment may temporarily serve to protect society (a point, by the way, which can be disputed), in the long run society is worse off for having imprisoned the convict. Furthermore, since prisons constitute part of society as a whole, the violence which occurs within them should figure into the tabulations of violence which occur in the society at large; prisons merely serve to displace the violence from *us* to *them*— for the time being.

Prison sentences are also designed to function as sheer punishment or retribution, independently of their deterrent, protective, or rehabilitative effects. Whether or not this is a proper function of prison is a moral, and perhaps a Constitutional, issue beyond the scope of this book; but from a psychological perspective, the imposition of punishment for retributive purposes is highly interwoven with its other stated functions. By being retributive and punitive, "the system" encourages retribution and punishment by the population at large. Since nearly everyone imprisoned is ultimately released, the question of who is punished in the long run is worth considering.

Finally, prison sentences, as well as other forms of punishment, are designed to make individuals accept responsibility for their behavior. This function is well-served by penalties for criminal conduct. Even though I have argued that much violence is instigated by situational variables, such as opportunity and other features of the physical and social environment, it is nonetheless true that people exercise a choice in placing themselves in certain kinds of situations. Exposure to "temptation" may facilitate criminal acts, but to the extent that people place themselves in situations where temptation and opportunity are maximal, they should accept responsibility for their behavior (even if the behavior would also have been engaged in by anyone else under similar circumstances). While criminal sanctions do hold individuals responsible for their behavior, the law recognizes that occasionally environmental pressures exerted on an actor are so potent that the actor should not be held accountable for his behavior; two such legally acceptable means of absolving an aggressor's responsibility are the "temporary insanity" plea and the self-defense or justifiable homicide defenses.

What is evident from the preceding discussion is that punishment fails to serve at least three of its primary functions—rehabilitation, protection, and deterrence. Much of this failure can be placed on the long delay in bringing cases to a conclusion, but much of it as well resides in the nature of imprisonment. Most important for the present purposes is to indicate that punishment, if it is to serve to reduce criminal violence must follow as soon as possible the act it is designed to reduce, and must also prevent influencing the convict's values, attitudes and behavior to the long-term detriment of society and the convict.

Short-term changes in the criminal justice system, which includes the police, the courts and corrections, are suggested later in this chapter.

REDUCING CRIME BY REDUCING CRIMES

If we examine the role of the police as potential deterrents to crime, we immediately become entangled in a complex network of police duties, functions, attitudes, and values. The police act as traffic regulators, social workers, lawyers, a lost-and-found, bicycle and taxicab registrars, escorts, enforcers of law, and society's "moral guardians."

Over half of all arrests made by the police in the United States involve what are typically referred to as "victimless crimes," that is, crimes which involve no personal or property damage or loss to anyone other than the offender* (drunkenness, vagrancy, sex and narcotic law violations, gambling, and so on). These victimless crimes accounted for over four million arrests in 1971, nearly two and one-half times the number of arrests for "serious crimes," those seven crimes which the F.B.I. considers serious in its Uniform Crime Reports: murder, aggravated assault, forcible rape, robbery, burglary, larceny, and auto theft.

It is highly questionable whether the victimless crimes should occupy police involvement at all, not so much on the grounds that they involve arbitrary standards of morality as on the grounds that they prevent the police from performing other, more essential duties and may, in fact, undermine respect for the law and its agents.

The police insist that they are simply enforcing existing laws in prosecuting victimless crimes, but it has been argued that the

---

* While there is widespread agreement that gambling, sex, and narcotics violations constitute victimless crimes, the term is not without its ambiguities. Laws regulating such behavior undoubtedly viewed "society" or the "common good" as the victims of such crimes. So the term "victimless crimes" as commonly used is value-laden, and we might more properly consider gambling, sex and narcotics violations simply as more acceptable to many people today than when the laws prohibiting them were passed.

police do not enforce all laws nor prosecute all suspects equally,[22] which may weaken support for, and cooperation with, the police in the community of the prosecuted. For example, the kinds of crime considered serious by the F.B.I. may be perceived by the poor as efforts at harassment since crimes committed by the wealthy are not pursued by the police with the same vigor, or are not considered sufficiently serious to warrant prosecution. As Jessica Mitford[23] notes: "Absent from the Uniform Crime Reports are crimes committed by the rich and powerful against the rest of the population: murder, assault, and theft via violation of health and safety codes by slum landlords, mine owners, construction companies, robbery by the food industry through deceptive packaging, and organized crime that depends on corruption of public officials, to name a few." Also, the types of victimless crimes enforced by the police are those in which minorities and the poor are likely to be overrepresented; if they are not overrepresented among offenders, they are certainly overrepresented among those prosecuted. A black man who is drunk will more often than not be booked on a drunkenness or disorderly conduct charge and be kept overnight in jail, while a white who is drunk is likely to be driven home by the police.

Alcoholism and other forms of drug abuse are serious and socially disruptive medical and psychological problems; the law compounds this by making them legal problems first and foremost. While some have argued that individuals have the right to do with their bodies as they see fit, our concern here is not so much with what ultimate treatment—if any—alcoholics, narcotic addicts, homosexuals, and prostitutes should receive, but with the fact that prosecution of such persons has important implications for various forms of criminality. The prosecution of crimes of morality impedes the police and other law enforcement agencies from pursuing more serious kinds of crime, such as violent, business, political, and property crime which have widespread effects on large numbers of people, and is seen as arbitrary and capricious by the groups most often prosecuted, the young and the poor. This leads to unfavorable attitudes toward the police, resentment and distrust of them, and failure to cooperate with them, all of which reduce the overall effectiveness of the law as an instrument of social control and of law enforcement agents as deterrents to crime.

In the past several years there has been increasing pressure to legalize a variety of victimless crimes. The repeal of laws making offenses of gambling, marijuana and narcotics use, pornography, and prostitution and other sexual acts between adults has been called for, usually on the grounds that since so many people violate the existing laws, fair and impartial law enforcement is impossible. Morris and Hawkins[24] argue that the "overreach" of the law may *contribute* to crime by creating inflated prices for confiscated items, such as narcotics, which fosters organized crime and exposes the police to bribes. Also, police should be freed from duties such as directing traffic, writing parking tickets, registering bicycles and taxis, running ambulance services, and rescuing stranded cats from trees.

Heroin and Crime: A Fix in Time Saves Nine

It is impossible to determine the precise number of heroin addicts in the United States, but estimates of their number range from 60,000 to over 200,000. In order to maintain their narcotics habit, they must each spend from twenty-five to well over one hundred dollars a day on heroin. The means by which these vast sums of money are obtained are largely through selling drugs to others, stealing, prostitution, forgery, and, occasionally, mugging.[25] Over 10 per cent of all arrests for nondrug offenses involve drug addicts.[26]

Largely responsible for the criminal behavior of drug addicts —particularly robbery—has been our unwillingness as a nation to deal with drug addicts on any but a criminal level. Only when drug abuse became widespread in nonghetto areas of our cities was any concern shown for educative and rehabilitative programs, and even then there was great resistance to stripping away the criminal label and sanctions associated with addiction. The consequences of our failure to dissociate drugs from criminality has served to maintain and strengthen the link between the two. Stachnik[27] has discussed the undesirable effects of criminal penalties for drug use, which include undermining the stability of the user's family, reluctance of the addict to seek treatment, undermining respect for the law, maintaining an inflated price for heroin, exerting pressure on the addict to enlist new addicts, maintaining organized crime, inhibiting research on drug effects and treatment of addiction, and causing death and disease through the sale of adulterated drugs and the use of unsterilized paraphernalia. "It is probably not an exaggeration," according to Stachnik, "to say that if one set out to design a system guaranteed to continually increase the rate of addiction, our present system would be somewhere near optimal."

In order to envision the consequences of our present means of dealing with drug addiction, an example taken from Lessard[28] will be instructive. Imagine that the 200,000 diabetics in the United States were suddenly informed that insulin was illegal and that there were severe penalties for possession, sale, or use of insulin. Would they become less dependent on insulin? Would they stop injection of insulin because it was criminal? The probable effects of such a law would be to create an underground network of manufacture, distribution, and sale of insulin, not unlike the present heroin underworld. The price of insulin on the black market would rise dramatically, requiring the addict to obtain large sums of money, large enough to force him or her into further criminal activities in many cases. In time, the insulin addict would be indistinguishable from our present-day heroin addict.

Diabetics are currently indistinguishable from the rest of the population; they manage to support their families, to hold jobs, and to avoid the stigma of being labeled dangerous criminals, largely because insulin is freely available to them at reasonable cost. It is proposed that a system be developed, not very different from the British system of heroin maintenance, which would (1) remove criminal penalties for the possession and use of all drugs, (2) provide methadone or heroin to any addict upon request, and (3) provide educational, psychological, and occupational therapy upon request. Far from costing more money than our present system, the proposed maintenance and therapeutic system would be far less costly in terms of manpower needs. It would save lives by eliminating accidental overdoses, check the spread of drug-related diseases, such as hepatitis and septicemia, and enable the addict to dissociate himself or herself from a criminal underworld. These in turn would reduce urban crime by anywhere from 15 to 50 per cent, and, according to Stachnik, "perhaps most important, for the first time some contact between a benign 'establishment' and the heroin subculture would be firmly established."[29]

ADDITIONAL SHORT-TERM REMEDIES IN THE CRIMINAL JUSTICE SYSTEM

The criminal justice system consists of three sometimes-interrelated subsystems: the police, the courts, and corrections. Short-term changes in these institutions are presented separately, but in general the suggestions as a whole are designed to reduce discretionary powers in the system and to maximize equity and unbiased treatment of suspects, defendants, and convicts. Underlying these suggestions is the notion that *a generally positive attitude toward the law and law enforcement is more likely to deter crime than the particular threats and penalties which might emanate from the system.*

The Police

The President's Commission on Law Enforcement and Administration of Justice had a number of suggestions for improving police effectiveness and impartiality, some of which are consistent with the psychological principles and research presented in earlier chapters of this book. Included among their thirty-five recommendations are the following:

> Establish community relations units in departments serving substantial minority population.
> Establish citizen advisory committees in minority-group neighborhoods.
> Recruit more minority-group officers.
> Emphasize community relations in training and operations.
> Provide adequate procedures for processing citizen grievances against all public officials.
> Recruit more actively, especially on college campuses and in inner cities.
> Increase police salaries, especially maximums, to competitive levels.
> Set as goal, requirement of baccalaureate degree for general enforcement officers.
> Stress ability in promotion.
> Develop and enunciate policy guidelines for exercise of law enforcement discretion.
> Establish strong internal investigation units in all departments to maintain police integrity.
> Experiment with team policing combining patrol and investigative duties.
> Adopt policy limiting use of firearms by officers.[30]

Others have called for similar measures.[31] The psychological consequences of such measures would be to reduce the social distance between the police and the community at large by removing some of the discretionary powers which the police now have. This may be accomplished by setting official limits on acceptable police conduct and by providing citizens with a nonpolice grievance board. (Internal police investigation units would ensure that citizens who lodged formal complaints against police officers would not be harassed.) Additional measures which would reduce the intrusiveness of the police would be to reinstate foot patrols and simultaneously reduce the number of patrol cars in

any given neighborhood and to require policemen to live in the
neighborhoods to which they are assigned.

The Courts

Nearly forty specific recommendations for changes in the operations of the court system were made by the President's Commission on Law Enforcement and Administration of Justice, and a
number of others have called for a variety of changes in the
structure and operation of the courts:

> Increase judicial manpower.
> Enact comprehensive state bail reform legislation.
> Establish station house release and summons procedure.
> Revise sentencing provisions of penal codes.
> Establish probation services in all courts for presentence inves-
>   tigation of every offender.
> Institute procedures for promoting just and uniform sentencing.
> Institute timetable for completion of criminal cases.[32]

Two additional changes can be recommended: elimination of
the indeterminate sentence and elimination of secretive plea-
bargaining.

These suggestions for uniform sentencing procedures are designed to ensure speedy trials and to eliminate the biases now
built into the present court system against the indigent. For
example, wealthy defendants are easily able to arrange bail
while awaiting trial, while the poor must await trial in jail.[33]
Mitford[34] summarizes the statistics from the Federal Bureau of
Prisons records which "show that in 1970 the average sentence
for whites was 42.9 months, compared to 57.5 months for nonwhites. Whites convicted of income tax evasion were committed
for an average of 12.8 months and nonwhites for 28.6 months.
In drug cases, the average for whites was 61.1 months and for
nonwhites, 81.1." The need to revise sentencing provisions for
criminal violations can also be seen in the wide variety of
special-interest laws enacted in local and state legislatures and

in the vast discrepancies in sentences from one locality to another for the same offense. In Colorado, for example, a person convicted of first-degree murder must serve at least 10 years before becoming eligible for parole, while a person convicted of second-degree murder must serve at least 15 years before becoming eligible for parole. In the same state, stealing a dog is punishable by up to 10 years' imprisonment, while killing a dog is punishable by no more than 6 months' imprisonment.[35] Courts and laws which deal unevenly and prejudicially toward large segments of the population diminish respect for law in general and thereby foster crime.

Corrections

Perhaps no area of the criminal justice system is in as much need of revision as correctional facilities. As I have discussed earlier, prison sentences are not necessarily rehabilitative, and in the long run they may even fail to protect the society from crime.

Mitford has suggested that the very nature of prison may be such as to preclude long-term rehabilitation. The role of prisoner may be dehumanizing to the extent that true efforts at rehabilitation are unlikely or unable to succeed. Indeed, Haney, Banks, and Zimbardo[36] have shown in their study of a simulated prison that both guards and prisoners are influenced more by the total context of prison, that is, by their expectations of what prisons are and what happens in them, than by the specific attitudes and personalities of either guards or inmates. In their study, men were randomly assigned to be either prisoners or prison guards. Within only a few days the experiment had to be terminated because of the excessive abuse to which "prisoners" were exposed at the hands of the "guards."

While revisions are discussed more fully in Chapter 6, several necessary remedial steps should be taken to ensure that, at the very least, correctional institutions do not serve to teach and reinforce antisocial behavior. Karl Menninger,[37] in his elegant plea for prison reform, *The Crime of Punishment,* relates:

In G. K. Chesterton's *The Club of Queer Trades,* a judge must pass sentence on a prisoner at the bar: "I sentence you to three years' penal servitude, in the firm and God-given conviction that what you really require is three weeks at the sea-side."

While prison reform has repeatedly been called for over the past hundred years, no successful efforts to deal humanely with convicts have ever been instituted on a wide scale. As a necessary beginning, the adversary nature of the institution must be eliminated. Prisoners working in conjunction with administrators and other prison and community personnel must be made to feel a part of the society at large rather than apart from it. By assigning at least some of the responsibility for rehabilitation to the prisoners themselves, commitment to acceptable social behavior will be increased. Prisoners, not unlike the rest of us, resist influence attempts directed at their behavior which are imposed by external agents, particularly if those agents are seen as arbitrary or hostile. Furthermore, prison administrators must have available a variety of positive incentives for prisoners to encourage acceptable forms of social behavior, rather than the presently existing punishments consisting primarily of isolation and parole denials for antisocial conduct.[38] A variety of supportive facilities are required for prisoners, such as job training, education, and psychological counseling. Prison facilities should be small, community-based operations and should use the support facilities available in the surrounding community whenever possible. Rather than isolating the prisoner from his or her family, efforts should be taken to strengthen the family structure in the form of graduated release programs and expanded furlough programs. At present, only 5 per cent of the total prison budget is for rehabilitative services. This figure should be increased to a much larger proportion of the prison budget.

These reforms are hardly original, since they—or reforms like them—have been called for almost since prisons began. As Mitford has shown, however, they have never been instituted. One reason for resistance may be that prisons are so crowded with such a great variety of offenders that reform efforts seem secondary to the more mundane requirements of housing, feeding, and controlling the large number of people. The Board of Directors of the National Council on Crime and Delinquency has recently suggested that this problem be alleviated by providing "nondangerous offenders" with sentences not involving prison.[39] They have urged the courts to use treatment by appropriate social agencies, probation, suspended sentences, "deferred conviction," fines, restitution, boarding homes, and half-way houses as alternatives to prison sentences for all those convicted of crimes other than serious personal and organized crimes. That such programs are feasible can be seen from the fact that even prison administrators agree that *between 75 and 90 per cent of all prisoners would, if freed immediately, present no danger or threat to the community.*[40] This is consistent with the literature (discussed in Chapter 3) showing that most crimes, including personal crimes, are committed by relatively average people in rather atypical situations (rather than being committed by atypical people in normal situations).

SHORT-TERM INTERVENTION

While situational factors are seen largely as the determinants of aggression and crime, certain psychological traits of some individuals make them more likely to aggress in what I have called aggressible environments. Among the psychological characteristics are impulsivity, loss of cognitive control over behavior, deindividuation, inability to delay gratification, an extensive aggressive repertoire, and a restricted range of alternative, nonaggressive behaviors.

One way to curtail aggressive behavior is to structure the environment in such a way as to minimize the opportunity for aggression. However, since most violence is committed against persons familiar or friendly to the aggressor, no matter how the environment is altered, it would neither be possible—nor desirable—to minimize contact with familiar people or places, to in-state cognitive control over certain behavior, or to maximize mutual surveillance of some areas. Since cognitive controls are relaxed in a familiar environment and in the presence of familiar others, some probability of engaging in aggression is always present in these situations. In order to reduce this probability, it is required that individuals learn to maintain control over their behavior or have a wide range of behavioral alternatives in which to engage other than aggression.

Particularly important for a reduction in the future occurrence of criminal aggression is the provision of juveniles who have already shown signs of criminality or excessive violence with alternative behaviors. The types of training which may be expected to reduce antisocial behavior include increasing the individual's ability to foresee the consequences of his or her actions and increasing the ability to verbalize, rather than act out, his or her feelings. There are quite a large number of intervention studies with juvenile delinquents, and a sampling of such studies will be presented in order to indicate the variety of approaches which have met with success in reducing antisocial acts.

In one study,[41] chronically delinquent boys were taught to place themselves in the positions of other people by making a film in which they had to enact a variety of different roles. This role-taking procedure was designed to reduce the egocentrism of the experimental subjects. A placebo group made an animated film but did not engage in role-taking, and a control group made no film at all. The results of the study indicated that enacting the roles of a variety of others did reduce egocentrism. The experimental group did show a significant reduction in delinquent offenses in the eighteen months following the film-making exercise, while no such reduction in delinquency was observed for the placebo or the control group.

A study by Alexander and Parsons[42] involved the fostering of communication and negotiation skills among members of delinquents' families. Recidivism rates for delinquents in these experimental families were compared with those delinquents receiving client-centered family therapy, church-sponsored family counseling, or no treatment. The results of the study showed that the lowest recidivism rate (26 per cent) was for those delinquents who, along with their families, received instruction in communicating and negotiating, while the highest recidivism rate (73 per cent) was for those receiving the family counseling. The recidivism rates for the client-centered groups (47 per cent) and the no treatment groups (50 per cent) were about the same as the recidivism rate for the county as a whole (51 per cent). Hence, as the authors conclude, "it appears that family intervention programs may profitably be focused on changing family interaction patterns in the direction of increased clarity and precision of communication, increased reciprocity of communication and social reinforcement, and contingency contracting emphasizing equivalence of rights and responsibilities for all family members." One effect of the family intervention technique employed by Alexander and Parsons may have been, as in the Chandler study on role-taking, to increase the delinquents' ability to view things from the perspective of others. This would in turn decrease impulsivity and the tendency to engage in self-centered behavior.

The importance of communication in reducing antisocial behavior is further highlighted by Ostrom, Steele, Rosenblood, and Mirels[43]:

By the time a youth is labeled a "juvenile delinquent" by society, he is likely to have developed a resistance to the conventional means society uses to transmit values and encourage law-abiding behavior. The school teacher punishes him for misbehavior in the hallways and classrooms, the judge instructs him to "mend his ways," a probation officer counsels him to keep off the streets and avoid "bad" company, parents scold, and ministers preach. He has become an inert and unreceptive agent in this communication process. Treatment programs for the abatement of delinquent behavior which do not alter this communication pattern have little chance of being effective.

Ostrom and his colleagues conducted an intervention study with delinquents who had been placed on probation by the juvenile court. A variety of social psychological principles were applied. Leaders of the intervention groups were selected and trained so that they would be familiar with the delinquents' problems and life styles and could be easily identified with by the delinquents. The site for the study was selected so that it would not have negative associations or elicit anxiety among the delinquents. The study was conducted in a laboratory at Ohio State University. The subjects were recruited through the courts in such a way as to maximize each subject's feeling of choice: the subjects were told that they would be released from mandatory visits with parole officers if they agreed to serve as "consultants in a project designed to understand 'why kids get into trouble.'" Attendance at the experimental sessions was purely voluntary since, as the authors note, "making participation a compulsory requirement can destroy the effectiveness of influence attempts." The two-hour sessions were held weekly for two months. During the sessions, the subjects discussed delinquency, the consequences of delinquent acts, and alternative means of achieving the participants' personal goals. A variety of role playing procedures was used in which participants took the role of parents, arresting officers, victims, law breakers, judges, jailers, school teachers, gang leaders, and innocent bystanders. In order to increase the boys' commitment during these role playing sessions, videotape recordings were made which were viewed and discussed. The boys were rewarded with a letter of praise for behavior which was self-initiated and internally motivated. A control group of delinquents received no such treatment.

School and court records were examined during the ten months immediately following the experimental sessions, and at the end of this ten month follow-up, subjects were given a variety of paper and pencil measures to determine whether the treatment sessions had any lasting influence on values or attitudes. Nearly twice as many members of the control group (48 per cent) as the experimental group (26 per cent) committed at least one delinquent act during the ten months following the sessions. During the first four months after the sessions, 50 per cent of the control group, as compared to 8 per cent of the experimental group, had at least one arrest. The difference between the experimental and control groups diminished with the passage of time, indicating the need for longer-term intervention sessions or the occasional reinstatement of the treatment. Subjects in the experimental group, however, did show a lasting increase in self-supportive attitudes.

A number of intervention studies have altered the consequences of aggressive behavior by withholding rewards for aggression and by providing rewards for alternative, nonaggressive behavior.[44] While such studies have not been conducted on a large scale with groups of delinquents, they have been fairly successful in diminishing antisocial behavior among individuals. One of the bases for the Big Brother and Big Sister programs, in which a delinquent youth is paired with an older nondelinquent, usually a student, is that the Big Brother or Sister will serve as a model to the delinquent and will reward prosocial behavior while ignoring or disapproving of antisocial behavior.

While the various programs outlined above might reduce street crime, auto theft, or recidivism among criminals and deliquents, they leave untouched the basic core of aggression—the acquisition of aggressive and antisocial values, attitudes, and behaviors. The remedies suggested in this chapter are capable of reducing antisocial behavior among people who have already acquired a basic aggressive repertoire. However, without fundamental changes in the things which people learn and the ways in which they learn them, it is only a matter of time before the effectiveness of such remedial measures diminishes.

TOWARD ELIMINATION OF VIOLENCE

6

The citizens of this country, like their leaders, have little regard for human life and human dignity. They may never have engaged in overt acts of violence against other human beings; yet they support such acts, or at the very least are content to tolerate them without dissent.

Alphonso Pinkney[1]

The various suggestions for control of violence and crime proposed in the preceding chapter are not dramatically different from proposals made by others, such as the various Presidential commissions on violence and civil disorders.[2] However, they fail to come to grips with the core element of violence, that is, the widespread support given to violence in a number of our social institutions. If people did not learn violence, they would not be violent, regardless of the provocations to which they were exposed.* (My argument that the primary causes of aggression

---

* There is some important literature on the positive functions of violence which should be mentioned at this point. By stating that people would not engage in violence if they had not learned to be violent—even in the

are to be found in situational and environmental factors rests on the assumption that people have generally already acquired some basic aggressive capabilities.) If we are to begin to eliminate violence from the national scene, we will have to make changes in a variety of social institutions. We will be required to raise and educate our children differently, to prepare for the national defense differently, to change the ways in which we view the police, the courts, the prisons, the business community, politicians, and ourselves. The recommendations presented in Chapter 5 would result in minor changes, additions, and corrections in a number of social institutions; those presented below call for reconstruction. As the President's Commission on Law Enforcement and Administration of Justice has noted[4]:

> Crime is a social problem that is interwoven with almost every aspect of American life; controlling it involves changing the way schools are run and classes are taught, the way cities are planned and built, the way businesses are managed and workers are hired. Crime is a kind of human behavior; controlling it means changing the minds and hearts of men. Controlling crime is the business of every American institution. Controlling crime is the business of every American.

---

face of extreme provocation—the issue of whether violence or violation of the law, as in civil disobedience, is ever justified, is raised. Certainly there are deprivations and injustices imposed on individuals and groups by others, and violence often appears to be the only way out of such intolerable situations. In fact, as stated in our definition of aggression, the imposition of psychological (or physical) harm on another is in itself aggressive. My purpose here is not to become embroiled in the philosophical discussions of whether violence or civil disobedience is ever justified, but to stress that violence can sometimes serve positive social functions (although these functions may be better served via other means). Violence can serve as a danger signal to others, to warn those in power or authority that the individual or group engaged in violence is in need of help. The riots which occurred in various United States ghettoes in the 1960's served just such a function, and juvenile delinquency and near-suicides have also been interpreted as "cries for help."[3]

REMOVING REWARDS FOR VIOLENCE
AND THE LEARNING OF AGGRESSION

Three essential forms of learning aggression were discussed in Chapter 2: classical conditioning, operant conditioning, and modeling and imitation. If society is to apply these learning approaches to the elimination of violence, it will become necessary to condemn rather than praise violence (classical conditioning), to remove rewards for violence (operant conditioning), and to minimize the number of models of aggressive behavior in the social environment (modeling and imitation).

Those with vested interests, who stand to profit in some way from violence will, intentionally or otherwise, act in such a way as to produce the self-interested behavior. This applies equally to street gangs in the ghetto, for whom violence serves as a means to a reputation, and to organized crime and weapons industries, for whom violence provides monetary rewards. Violence at all levels must thus become unprofitable and undesirable. Material and social profit must be eliminated from institutions which deal in violence, and alternate, nonviolent, means for individual achievement and recognition must be provided. The National Commission on the Causes and Prevention of Violence clearly recognized that violence was often employed to obtain "social justice." The Commission stated: "To make violence an unnecessary tactic, our institutions must be capable of providing political and social justice for all who live under them and of correcting injustice against any group by peaceful and lawful means. . . . We cannot 'insure domestic tranquility' unless we 'establish justice'—in a democratic society, one is impossible without the other."[5]

There are a number of ways in which the reward structure in relation to violence can be altered. One is to increase the personal costs of violent behavior, primarily through public condemnation of violence[6]; another is to decrease the positive reinforcements for engaging in violence; and a third is to provide alternative ways of arriving at desirable goals without the need to resort to violence.

THE FAMILY AND SCHOOL: PARENT-REARING

We have seen in Chapter 2 that the underlying core of aggressive behavior and related attitudes, values, and norms are acquired during childhood and that the greatest influence on this learning is the behavior of parents. Parents who praise aggression in at least some forms, parents who directly or inadvertently reward aggressive behavior, and parents who themselves are aggressive teach their children to be aggressive. When parents also show a lack of affection, concern, and understanding toward their children, such learning will be even more pronounced.

Several of the short-term intervention studies mentioned in the previous chapter show that when parents of delinquent youth are provided with a few simple skills, such as how to correctly reward and punish behavior and how to exchange ideas and feelings with their children, improvements in the children's behavior soon follow. But it is not only the parents of delinquent youth who need to learn child-rearing skills; most parents teach their children at least some antisocial behaviors and values, and often do so inadvertently.

Some of the major elements of successful child rearing have historically been present in most families: tenderness, affection, concern, understanding. But also present in most families were inconsistencies in behavior, the modeling of aggression and praise for particular instances of aggression, which provided their offspring, if not with propensities to engage in violence, at least with pro-aggression values and behaviors which would find expression under certain circumstances.

While high school and college courses are offered in automobile mechanics, the films of Bergman, volleyball, advertising, and cooking, none are offered in how to raise children. (This is not true of some countries, such as the Soviet Union, in which training in moral behavior, concern for family, and social skills are taught throughout the school system.[7]) Students should be provided with instruction, from grade school through high school, in the philosophy and psychology of parenthood. Such instruction need not be ideological, as is the Soviet teaching of social and moral skills, but it should provide students with an understanding of the functions of parenthood and with a variety of social and psychological skills which will enable them to raise their own children in an intelligent, purposive, and effective manner. Of course, since children learn many behaviors and values from their parents, the longer such training programs are in effect, the greater should be their positive effects. The first generation of parents formally trained in child-rearing skills will only be moderately effective in rearing their children since the parents will also have acquired a number of undesirable values and behaviors from their own parents. Each successive generation of trained parents should be able to more closely approximate their ideal child rearing goals.

Let us look at two examples which have been discussed earlier: punishment and child abuse. While parents are being taught means of coping with their children on a short-term basis in several pediatric hospitals and behavior therapy clinics in the United States, it should be a standard part of their education and more correctly belongs in the schools. Students can be instructed in the psychology of punishment so that they can decide for themselves whether, in a given situation, it would be advisable to punish their children. The learning of a variety of social skills, such as the communication of attitudes and emotional feelings, would provide the student with alternatives to physical punishment so that as parents they could teach their children what they wanted them to learn without inadvertently teaching them to be aggressive. Intervention does not take place until a parent has already battered a child; education concerning child rearing which occurs in the schools should prevent child abuse from arising in the first place.

Cases of child abuse could be sharply reduced if parents had available a variety of nonaggressive behaviors from which they could choose when dealing with their children. In many American cities, twenty-four hour crisis centers have been established for parents who simply do not know what to do with their children in a particular situation and who fear that they might harm them. They have only to call the center for counseling and expert advice. Although the effects of such centers on the child abuse rate are not known, it is likely that, by providing parents with one additional nonviolent alternative, they may be less likely to resort to physical abuse. Providing parents with a variety of nonpunitive behaviors from which they can choose in an aggression-provoking situation will reduce the tendency to resort to violence, since violence is frequently chosen as the behavior of last resort.

But it is not the parents alone who are responsible for children's moral and social development. The schools must serve as an appendage of the home in reinforcing the moral and social training provided by parents. This means that there must be some consistency between the moral and social training which the child receives at home and that which he or she receives in school. If parents and teachers are to be consistent in the behaviors, values, and attitudes they model and reinforce, there will have to be some general agreement between them on what those behaviors and moral principles should be. This can only be accomplished through cooperative contact and discussion between school administrators, teachers, and parents.

A note should be made here about sex differences and child rearing and learning. There is a growing awareness among teachers and parents that it is detrimental to children to teach them stereotypic sex role behavior. For example, it will not be to a girl's benefit to learn submission and passivity since, for example, this will undermine her later initiative in seeking an education and a career. The compensating tendency from this heightened awareness may be to train girls in the same way that boys have been trained previously. This would have the effect of increasing overt aggressiveness among future generations of women. Therefore, girls should not be reared as boys now are, but certain aspects of female socialization and of male socialization should be maintained. In other words, while sex differences in training should be minimized, both males and females should learn not to inhibit self-expression and at the same time learn to hold negative attitudes toward overt aggression.

The psychologist Nevitt Sanford, one of the authors of the classic *Authoritarian Personality,* has noted more recently that, "For turning our culture in the direction of humane and democratic values nothing is more important than reform of our schools. Nobody knows how this reform is to be accomplished, but we can offer some suggestions. Although schools probably need some structure, they certainly do not have to be authoritarian. The authoritarian style . . . is not inherent in human nature but is a patterned reaction to circumstances."[8] Therefore, at the same time that schools begin to teach positive social skills, they should also become less structured, so that children are given a more active and responsible role to play, the effects of which would be to instill in them a sense of independence and of accepting responsibility for their decisions.

THE MASS MEDIA: TOWARD A PUBLIC ACCOUNTABILITY

Violence in the mass media teaches pro-aggression values and behaviors and may, in specific instances, instigate individual acts of aggression. The most pernicious effect of media violence is probably the implicit support it lends to aggression by portraying fictional heroes as stronger than and as violent as villains and as justified in their use of violence. The same may be said of the media's emphasis on body contact sports. In the area of news reporting, the presentation, and particularly the sensationalization, of violence also teaches and may instigate individual acts of violence. There are a number of studies which bear out the statement that publicity given to violent acts can lead to subsequent criminal aggression. For example, Berkowitz and Macaulay[9] found that following both the assassination of President Kennedy in November 1963 and the multiple murders by Richard Speck and Charles Whitman in 1966 there were unusually sharp increases in the number of violent crimes committed. Further, Payne and Payne[10] reported a decrease in various crimes during a newspaper strike in Detroit, indicating that the reporting of crime might well stimulate future crimes.

There are some sensitive issues raised by these findings and by those reported in Chapter 2. On the one hand, since evidence indicates that violence in mass media serves in several ways to increase aggression and crime, then the elimination of violence in the media may act to reduce criminal violence. On the other hand, if certain media content are censored, they are apt to become more attractive and more valued by people[11]; and in any event, censorship is not an acceptable means of controlling media content in a democratic society. What may be done to minimize media portrayal of violence is to inform people of the media's effects, to insure efficient and impartial regulation of the media by the Federal Communications Commission (whose charter specifies that "the airwaves belong to the people . . ."), and to apply economic pressure to sponsors of violent media programming.

The National Commission on the Causes and Prevention of Violence recommended several years ago that "the broadcasting of children's cartoons containing serious non-comic violence should be abandoned. . . . The amount of time devoted to the broadcast of crime, western, and action-adventure programs containing violent episodes should be reduced."[12] That such voluntary actions have not been taken by the broadcast industry is indicated by a look at any television program guide. During the week of January 5, 1974, for example, three major commercial networks showed a total of 124 prime-time programs. Of this total, 24 were news programs and 38 were "crime dramas." The networks claim that they would not portray violent shows so frequently if they did not receive such high Nielsen ratings. The *TV Guide* reported the following:

It was the old, old rating story again: on the night of December 16, while more than two out of three TV homes across the country watched one of two regular crime-chasing dramas (39 per cent of the audience tuned in *Columbo,* another 29 per cent *Mannix*), a mere 26 per cent of the viewers chose to catch the rare TV appearance of Katherine Hepburn in ABC's critically applauded "The Glass Menagerie." . . .[13]

What the networks and the above report fail to take into account are two factors. First, if people are accustomed to watching immense quantities of violence on television, then they will come to prefer violent programs; and second, if people are apathetic about what they view on TV, they might simply choose at random which programs to watch. The ratings referred to in the *TV Guide* report reflect very much a random distribution which indicates no particular preference at all (we would expect, given three major networks, that about one-third of the viewers would watch each network).

What is of utmost importance for the future is that the television audience be provided with a wider choice in programming and that program content more adequately reflect the will of the true owners of the television airwaves—not American Home Products; Colgate-Palmolive; General Foods, Mills, or Motors; Lever Brothers; or Proctor and Gamble, but the American public. A variety of proposals for effective influence of the mass media have been presented by F.C.C. commissioner Nicholas Johnson in his book, *How to Talk Back to Your Television Set.*[14]

The mass media should depict, not only fewer acts of antisocial behavior, but a greater number of acts of a prosocial nature. There is considerable research evidence that not only do people learn and imitate the antisocial behavior which they observe on television and in movies, but also learn and imitate the prosocial behavior which they see. In fact, simply increasing the number of programs depicting positive forms of social behavior may in itself reduce the negative effects of aggressive programming.[15]

With respect to the reporting of *factual events* in the mass media, several recommendations can be made. The most important is to present criminal and violent behavior in such a way that it does not appear to be desirable, justified, or without serious consequences. One step which can be taken along these lines is to report such acts in units which are meaningful in terms of their human significance. For example, the confiscation of heroin during a narcotics raid should not be reported in terms of the weight of the heroin but in terms of the number of addicts who might have used that heroin; it most certainly should not be reported in terms of its dollar value in street sales, which most often is inflated in any case. Bombing raids, such as those which took place during the Vietnam war, should not have been reported in terms of "missions" or "sorties" or "megatons" of bombs, but in units which indicate how many people were killed, or the area of inhabited land bombed, or even in terms of the cost in dollars per taxpayer. Reporting bombing raids in tonnages or sorties is designed to obscure; reporting heroin in dollar value units is designed to impress. The units should indicate the human and social consequences of the acts described. Implicit in these remarks is the recognition that there is a variety of ways in which facts may be reported; I am simply arguing that the descriptions chosen to present such facts be consistent with the public interest.

There are good psychological reasons behind the use of such labels which can best be shown in an example by the Yale psychologist, Irving Janis, in which he describes decision-making during the Lyndon Johnson administration:

. . . when the in-group of key advisers met with Johnson every Tuesday, their meetings were characterized by a games theory detachment concerning the consequences of the war policies they were discussing. The members of this group adopted a special vocabulary for describing the Vietnam war, using terms such as body counts, armed reconnaissance, and surgical strikes, which they picked up from their military colleagues. The Vietnam policy makers, by using this professional military vocabulary, were able to avoid in their discussions with each other all direct references to human suffering and thus to form an attitude of detachment similar to that of surgeons. But although an attitude of detachment may have functional value for those who must execute distressing operations, it makes it all too easy for policy makers to dehumanize the victims of war and to resort to destructive military solutions without considering their human consequences.[16]

The labels with which one thinks about events come to have a strong influence on *what* one thinks about them. It is a telling sign of our national attitude that, instead of "making peace" with ourselves, we "wage wars" on poverty and crime. By employing such a phrase, it is easy to think of poverty and crime in terms of us (the wagers of war) and them (not only poverty and crime, per se, but also the "carriers" of poverty and crime).

REDUCING INSTITUTIONALIZED MODELING OF AGGRESSION

In the same way that rewards for aggression portrayed in the mass media foster aggression and related values, so too does antisocial behavior committed by those prominent in public affairs. Aggression and criminal behavior by those in the upper social strata strengthen and instigate similar acts by others in the society. Recently, for example, the mayor of a large American city admitted at a press conference that he had members of the local police department assemble dossiers on local judges. When asked whether that wasn't a violation of the Constitution, he answered that, even if it was, he would continue to have the police maintain the dossiers.[17] Such blatant disregard for the law can only reduce respect for the law among observers in less prestigious social positions. Likewise, the political scandals in Washington during the early 1970's, involving officials in the highest levels of government, have undermined respect for the law and thereby have increased the likelihood that other citizens will engage in criminal activities.

It is not only government officials involved in criminal activities who lend support to criminality; what has generally been referred to as business- or white-collar-crime also reinforces and sets examples for other types of illegal conduct. The extent of such crime, while it is difficult to determine precisely, far exceeds in economic and social impact the more readily detectable forms of street crime reported by the F.B.I. in its annual Uniform Crime Reports. In their criminology text, Bloch and Geis[18] discuss the varieties of white-collar crime, ranging from advertising fraud, violations of anti-trust legislation, and income tax evasion, to overcharges on automobile, electrical appliances, and watch repairs. In a classic study of business crime, E. H. Sutherland[19] examined the top seventy corporations in the United States and found that nearly one thousand adverse decisions had been rendered against them by courts or administrative bodies, with at least one decision against each of the seventy corporations.

> Financial losses due to white-collar crime, Sutherland pointed out, are probably many times as great as the financial cost of all acts customarily included in the so-called "crime problem." An officer of a chain grocery store, for instance, embezzled $600,000 in one year, a figure six times higher than the annual losses from five hundred robberies and burglaries in the stores in that chain. Million-dollar burglaries or robberies are virtually unknown, and constitute national sensations, where a million-dollar embezzlement is a rather routine event.

The question has been raised by some legal scholars, as well as by some criminologists, whether white-collar crimes should be considered crimes at all. They hold that many white-collar crimes involve torts, or infractions of the civil law, rather than violations of the criminal law. I would argue that, while there may be legal and historical reasons to distinguish between white-collar and personal crimes, there is less psychological justification to do so. Any action which an individual chooses to perform and which is designed to injure, physically or psychologically, another person is an aggressive act. We have not previously distinguished between aggressive acts which are legal and those which are illegal, nor between those which are direct (physical) and those which are indirect (psychological); they differ largely in degree and are essentially similar in other respects. The fact that one man accosts another on the street in order to obtain his money, while a second sells Florida swampland as an "ideal spot for a vacation home" in order to obtain the buyer's money does not make one actor significantly less aggressive than the other. While some acts of aggression are legal and others illegal, I have chosen to treat them in a similar fashion. One further reason for treating them together is because it can be argued that the amount of legal aggression which exists in a society is highly related to the amount of illegal violence which exists. The more tolerant a society is of various kinds of acceptable (legal) violence, as in play, humor, sports, politics, entertainment, and daily social intercourse, the more likely it will be to have high rates of criminal violence since the former serve largely as training grounds for the latter. If a society is saturated with petty violence, it is sure to have a high degree of criminal violence as well; and if a society is saturated with criminal behavior among its ruling elite, it will be flooded with crime among its masses.

Public concern over crime is generally restricted to those crimes which are reflected in the Uniform Crime Reports of the F.B.I. Listed as "serious crimes" in the reports are murder, forcible rape, robbery, aggravated assault, burglary, larceny (fifty dollars and over), and auto theft. These are, of course, matters which should concern the public, and the police; but many crimes committed on less personal bases, such as white-collar crimes, are no less (perhaps even more) serious in their consequences. If the Unifom Crime Reports are maintained in the future and if they are to be used as an index of crime in the United States, then they should accurately reflect the spectrum of crime, including those committed by middle- and upper-class citizens in addition to those committed by the poor, young, and nonwhite.

The Uniform Crime Reports rely on those crimes which are reported to the police, and therefore, they are highly dependent upon the willingness of citizens to report crime and on the accounting methods used by the varoius police departments across the nation. A more accurate index of the extent of crime would be obtained from interviews conducted with nationwide random samples of citizens. Of primary importance is that the public and law enforcement agencies expand their conception of and concern about crime to encompass the whole range of serious infringements on individual and social liberties.

MILITARISM IN THE UNITED STATES

One index of the national attitude toward violence is the size and pervasiveness of our military establishment. The American budget for national defense is currently about 90 billion dollars a year; that amounts to about $1000 per taxpayer per year. Nearly every segment of the American economy is dependent upon military funds of one sort or another. In 1973, when the Defense Department announced that, as an economy measure, it would close a number of military installations throughout the country, there was considerable resistance from local and state government officials based on the expected economic consequences of the cutbacks. Tristram Coffin has estimated that 70 per cent of the scientific research in the United States is done directly or indirectly for the Pentagon.[20] In 1964, Coffin wrote that "taxpayer groups and congressmen are suspicious of welfare payments, but no responsible citizen complains of turning over more than fifty billion dollars annually [the number has since nearly doubled] to the military establishment."

That the military is firmly entrenched in the national economy can be seen by their request for increased funds for the 1975-76 fiscal year. Note that the request was made despite the prediction of the National Commission on the Causes and Prevention of Violence that "the end of the Vietnam war should reduce defense expenditures by nineteen billion dollars annually."[21]

For the past thirty years, the primary concerns of American government have been the national defense, the growth of the economy and, more recently, the conquest of space. These concerns have used up over two-thirds of all federal and about one-half of local and state expenditures. The need to place social and human concerns higher in the list of national priorities is well-known and generally agreed upon by the public. It is probably the case that resistance to the reordering of national priorities comes primarily from those with vested economic interests in the current state of affairs. Increased expenditures for education, social security, welfare, medical treatment, housing, and urban planning, however, might well fall under the heading of national defense.

There are at least three ways in which our government spending for social and human needs may serve foreign policy and national defense goals. First, much of our foreign policy is conducted under the assumption that nations, like people, have motives, desires, abilities, attitudes, and values. If this is so, then as a nation we should attempt to provide a model for other nations to emulate. One example of modeling by nations can be seen in the influence of the Scandinavian countries on the domestic and foreign affairs of other nations, which is far disproportionate to their size, and certainly disproportionate to their budgets for military hardware. Those opponents of American foreign aid who base their criticism on the ground that those we assist do not respect us, are essentially correct in one regard: friendship cannot be purchased, it must be earned. Second, if our government attended more fully to the needs of its citizens, internal threats to the government would diminish. By officially enacting policies which encompass egalitarian and compassionate principles, public officials would not only reduce incentives for crime, but would also serve as behavioral models for other citizens. Third, if we reduced military expenditures, the probability of a "hot" war would diminish correspondingly. Fredric Wertham illustrates the point:

> Another obstacle (to peace) is the idea so taken for granted today; if you want peace, prepare for war. . . . We have had a chance for almost 2,000 years to test this principle. It has never been true in all of history. Far more true is the African

proverb: "A newly sharpened sword marches by itself to the next village." If we want peace, we must prepare for *peace*.[22]

These three reasons for reordering our national goals are based essentially on two psychological principles discussed in Chapters 2 and 3. The first principle is that people learn from the behavior of others as well as imitate that behavior. By minimizing our aggressive military posture and by increasing our concern for the welfare and rights of citizens, we can expect comparable changes to occur in the behavior of some other nations. The genuine display of concern will be learned and imitated not only by other countries, but also by individuals within them and within our own country as well. The second principle concerns the use of weapons of destruction: the more widespread and abundant weapons are, the greater the probability that they will be used. Buttons seductively invite a push.

There is not room here to discuss the psychological foundations of military defense, and in any case that has been done admirably by others.[23] It is important, however, to indicate that our national priorities must be reorganized if we are to come to grips with the internal problems of crime and aggression and that, by minimizing spending for military weaponry, our nation can be stronger and less vulnerable than it is presently.

INSTITUTING SOCIAL CHANGE

In order to curtail crime in the immediate future and to prevent its occurrence in the long run, it will be necessary to change our current ways of conceptualizing it and of dealing with it. In the same way that parents and teachers must acquire new techniques for training children, so too must people in general acquire new standards of interaction with one another, and particularly with those whose behavior is at variance with prevailing standards.

When prison reforms are discussed there is usually an objection raised on the grounds that the convict has offended society and does not deserve to be treated compassionately. Never mind

that convicts are almost always young or poor or black; there is
something besides ageism and racism in the resistance to reform.
Our institutions designed to deal with the mentally ill, with abandoned and orphaned children, and with the aged are not terribly
different from those designed to deal with convicts. And there is
resistance to reform these institutions as well.

One source of this reluctance to expend public resources on
reform and of the failure to exert pressure for adequate facilities
and treatment of these social outcasts can be partially traced to a
mechanism of psychological denial. It is disturbing to think
about prisoners, orphans, the mentally ill, and old folks because,
at one and the same time, they are not very different from the
rest of us and yet they are so very different from the rest of us.
To dwell on them is to recognize that the boundary which sepa-
rates us from them is thin and fragile. One of the mechanisms by
which that boundary can be widened is to isolate those we find
offensive or threatening to our well-being and thereby rid our
thoughts of them. On the other hand, if we are to decrease their
numbers it will be necessary to deal with them directly and ultimately to return them to the social community.

In the case of prisons, nearly all convicts do return to the community. If former convicts are to live crime-free lives it will be
necessary to provide them with the opportunities and skills to
do so. At the present time there are few organizations designed
to facilitate the reintegration of ex-convicts into society, and
those which do exist, such as the Fortune Society, are funded
and administered primarily by other ex-convicts. Public concern
for the reintegration of convicts is practically nonexistent.

From the standpoint of the felon a successful postprison life is
more than merely staying out of prison. From the criminal ex-
convict perspective it must contain other attributes, mainly it
must be dignified. This is not generally understood by correctional people whose ideas of success are dominated by narrow
and unrealistic conceptions of nonrecidivism and reformation.
Importantly, because of their failure to recognize the felon's
viewpoint, his aspirations, his conceptions of respect and dig-

nity, or his foibles, they leave him to travel the difficult route away from the prison without guidance or assistance; in fact, with considerable hindrance, and with few avenues out of a criminal life acceptable both to him and to his former keepers.[24]

The difficulty of leading a crime-free post-prison existence holds almost as much for those whose crimes were situationally caused as for those with heavy involvements in the underworld. This is the case because, as they now stand, prisons instill in the convict attitudes, values, and behaviors which favor violent behavior both in and out of prison.

If society is to continue to have prisons—and it is by no means clear that it should—several alterations in their use and structure are needed. Prison sentences should be given *only* when alternative means of treatment are unfeasible or prove unsuccessful. A variety of treatment and rehabilitation programs should be available to the courts to deal with first offenders. Such programs may involve small-scale community-based facilities with minimum restrictions placed on the convict's freedoms. These centers should be run by a consortium of government, community, and inmate leaders. The ultimate goal of alternative treatment facilities for those convicted of serious crimes should be the virtual elimination of traditional punitive means of "treatment." Since persons in these centers would be those who committed crimes of opportunity and circumstance, such centers should represent no threat to the community. Several important functions can be served by the establishment of nonpunitive treatment centers. First, by treating convicts with genuine concern for their welfare, corrections institutions serve as examples of values to be modeled by inmates as well as by individuals in the community. Second, recidivism will be reduced, protecting the community to which convicts eventually return. Third, they will provide convicts with alternative noncriminal means of reaching valued personal goals so that the motivation and opportunity for repetitive criminal behavior are reduced.

A number of proposals have been made in this and in the preceding chapter. Most of them have been made before by criminologists, judges, lawyers, and official investigative bodies of government. I have tried to supply the psychological justifications which exist for them, but I have not gone into much detail about their actual implementation. Naturally, whatever large-scale social reforms are attempted will need public and legislative support, but beyond this specific means of attaining social reform are absent. The reason for omitting such details is that the particular shape which our future institutions take will depend on a great variety of factors. For instance, I have suggested that punitive prison sentences be abolished and replaced with nonpunitive community treatment facilities. But such facilities can take a variety of forms, from simple dormitories where psychological counseling is provided to full-time residential centers containing classrooms, workshops, recreational facilities, and so on. In order to decide the best way to implement any social change, and in order to determine which changes are most likely to meet with success, it will be necessary to experiment with a number of alternative institutions. The federal government has within the past decade conducted a number of such experiments to determine the feasibility of various social reforms. The best-known such experiment is still underway. Sponsored by the United States Office of Economic Opportunity, a three-year experiment is being conducted to determine the effects of a negative income tax by employing a number of New Jersey families as a test sample. In much the same way, we now have available the statistical and research tools needed to conduct intelligent social reform experiments so that we may proceed in planning the future course which we would like society to take.[25]

NOTES

CHAPTER 1

1. L. Radzinowicz. *Ideology and crime.* N.Y.: Columbia University Press, 1966. P. 53.
2. K. Lorenz. *On aggression.* N.Y.: Harcourt, Brace & World, 1966. D. Morris. *The naked ape.* N.Y.: McGraw-Hill, 1967. R. Ardrey. *African genesis.* N.Y.: Dell, 1961; *The territorial imperative.* N.Y.: Atheneum, 1966.
3. S. Freud. Beyond the pleasure principle. Vol. 18 and Civilization and its discontents. Vol. 21. In J. Strachey, Ed., *The standard edition of the complete psychological works of Sigmund Freud.* London: Hogarth, 1955.
4. J. M. R. Delgado. Aggression and defense under cerebral radio control. In C. D. Clemente & D. B. Lindsley, Eds., *Aggression and defense: Neural mechanisms and social patterns.* Los Angeles: Univ. of California Press, 1967. Pp. 171-93; *Physical control of the mind.* N.Y.: Harpers, 1969.
5. K. Lorenz. Ritualized fighting. In J. D. Carthy & E. J. Ebling, Eds., *The natural history of aggression.* N.Y.: Academic Press, 1964. P. 49.
6. S. Binford. Apes and original sin. *Human Behavior,* 1972, *1* (6), 64-71. A. Alland, Jr. *The human imperative.* N.Y.: Columbia Univ. Press, 1972. M. F. A. Montagu. The new litany of "innate depravity," or original sin revisited. In M. F. A. Montagu, Ed., *Man and aggression.* N.Y.: Oxford Univ. Press, 1968. Pp. 3-17. T. C. Schneirla. In-

stinct and aggression. In M. F. A. Montagu, Ed., *Man and aggression*. Pp. 59-64. J. P. Scott. That old-time aggression. In M. F. A. Montagu, Ed., *Man and aggression*. Pp. 51-58.

7. Delgado. *Physical control of the mind.*

8. R. G. Heath. Electrical self-stimulation of the brain in man. *American Journal of Psychiatry*, 1963, *120*, 571-77.

9. K. E. Moyer. Brain research must contribute to world peace. In K. E. Moyer, Ed., *The physiology of hostility*. Chicago: Markham, 1971. Pp. 1-10. K. B. Clark. The pathos of power: A psychological perspective. *American Psychologist*, 1971, *26*, 1047-57.

10. J. M. R. Delgado. *Physical control of the mind*. Pp. 121-32 and J. P. Flynn. The neural basis of aggression in cats. In D. C. Glass, Ed., *Neurophysiology and emotion*. N.Y.: Rockefeller Univ. Press, 1967. Pp. 40-60.

11. V. H. Mark & F. R. Ervin. *Violence and the brain*. N.Y.: Harper & Row, 1970.

12. P. Jacobs, M. Brunton, & M. Melville. Aggressive behavior, mental sub-normality and the XYY male. *Nature*, 1965, *208*, 1351-52.

13. See L. F. Jarvik, V. Klodin, & S. S. Matsuyama. Human aggression and the extra Y chromosome. *American Psychologist*, 1973, *28*, 674-82. The same arguments can be made with regard to various kinds of brain damage as causes of aggression. Mark & Ervin (see Ref. 11 above) have reported brain-wave abnormalities among psychiatric patients with symptoms of excessive violence. Again, two facts must be kept in mind. First, not all people with brain-wave abnormalities (even of a specified type) commit violence, and, second, only a relatively small amount of violence is committed by those with detectable brain disorders.

14. N. E. Zinberg & G. A. Fellman. Violence: Biological need and social control. *Social Forces*, 1967, *45*, 533-41.

15. A. Storr. *Human aggression*. N.Y.: Bantam, 1970. R. May. *Power and innocence. A search for the source of violence*. N.Y.: Norton, 1972. E. Glover. *The roots of crime*. N.Y.: International Univ. Press, 1960.

16. Of the psychoanalytic hypotheses, the most controversial is the catharsis notion, which predicts that viewing or engaging in violence serves to discharge the observer's level of aggression. Some research has found support for such an idea (D. Bramel, B. Taub, & B. Blum. An observer's reaction to the suffering of his enemy. *Journal of Personality & Social Psychology*, 1968, *8*, 384-92. S. Feshbach & R. D. Singer. *Television and aggression*. San Francisco: Jossey-Bass, 1971. H. L. Fromkin, J. H. Goldstein & T. C. Brock. The role of "irrelevant" derogation in vicarious aggression catharsis: A field experi-

ment. Unpublished manuscript, Purdue Univ., 1973), while other research has failed to find evidence of catharsis (A. Bandura. Vicarious
processes: A case of no-trial learning. In L. Berkowitz, Ed., *Advances
in experimental social psychology*. Vol. 2, N.Y.: Academic Press,
1965. Pp. 1-55. L. Berkowitz. Experimental investigations of hostility
catharsis. *Journal of Consulting & Clinical Psychology*, 1970, *35*,
1-7). The catharsis concept is discussed more fully in Chapter 2.

17. E. G. Boring, H. S. Langfeld, & H. P. Weld. *Introduction to psychology*. N.Y.: Wiley, 1939. P. 163.

18. W. Goode. Violence among intimates. In D. J. Mulvihill & M. M.
Tumin, Eds., *Crimes of violence*. Washington, D.C.: U.S. Government Printing Office, 1969. P. 943.

19. G. Gorer. Man has no "killer" instinct. In M. F. A. Montagu, Ed.,
Man and aggression. Pp. 27-36.

20. N. Tinbergen. *The study of instinct*. Oxford: Clarendon, 1951.

21. L. Berkowitz. *Aggression: A social psychological analysis*. N.Y.:
McGraw-Hill, 1962.

22. J. Dollard, L. W. Doob, N. E. Miller, O. H. Mowrer, & R. R. Sears.
Frustration and aggression. New Haven: Yale Univ. Press, 1939.

23. A. H. Buss. Aggression pays. In J. L. Singer, Ed., *The control of aggression and violence*. N.Y.: Academic Press, 1971. Pp. 7-18.

24. K. E. Moyer. Kinds of aggression and their physiological bases.
Communications in Behavioral Biology, 1968, *2*(A), 65-87.

25. A similar type of model containing tendencies both for the expression
and the inhibition of aggression has recently been proposed by E. I.
Megargee. *The psychology of violence and aggression*. Morristown,
N.J.: General Learning Press, 1972.

26. The term norms is used here as a shorthand notation signifying
values, beliefs, attitudes, and expectations.

27. See the discussions by E. H. Sutherland & D. R. Cressey. *Principles
of criminology*. 7th Ed. Philadelphia: Lippincott, 1966. Pp. 77-83;
M. E. Wolfgang & F. Ferracuti. *The subculture of violence*. London:
Tavistock, 1967.

28. D. Byrne. Attitudes and attraction. In L. Berkowitz, Ed., *Advances
in experimental social psychology*. Vol. 4. N.Y.: Academic Press,
1969. Pp. 36-89.

29. E. Staub. The learning and unlearning of aggression: The role of
anxiety, empathy, efficacy, and prosocial values. In J. L. Singer, Ed.,
The control of aggression and violence. Pp. 93-124.

30. Cognitive dissonance theory makes comparable predictions, which
have received support in a number of studies. L. Festinger. *The
theory of cognitive dissonance*. Stanford, Calif.: Stanford Univ. Press,
1957. T. C. Brock & A. H. Buss. Dissonance, aggression, and evalu-

ation of pain. *Journal of Abnormal & Social Psychology*, 1962, *65*, 197-202.

CHAPTER 2

1. R. Wright. *Black boy*. N.Y.: Harper & Row, 1945. Pp. 70-71.
2. N. Morris & G. Hawkins. *The honest politician's guide to crime control*. Chicago: Univ. of Chicago Press, 1970.
3. S. Feshbach. Aggression. In P. H. Mussen, Ed., *Carmichael's manual of child psychology*. Vol. 2. N.Y.: Wiley, 1970.
4. I. P. Pavlov. *Conditioned reflexes*. N.Y.: Oxford Univ. Press, 1927.
5. J. Kagan & H. A. Moss. *Birth to maturity: A study in psychological development*. N.Y.: Wiley, 1962.
6. C. A. Loew. Acquisition of a hostile attitude and its relation to aggressive behavior. *Journal of Personality & Social Psychology*, 1967, *5*, 552-58.
7. R. G. Geen & R. R. Pigg. Acquisition of an aggressive response and its generalization to verbal behavior. *Journal of Personality & Social Psychology*, 1970, *15*, 165-70.
8. M. R. Yarrow, J. D. Campbell, & R. V. Burton. *Child rearing: An inquiry into research and methods*. San Francisco: Jossey-Bass, 1968.
9. See L. Berkowitz. The contagion of violence: An S-R mediational analysis of some effects of observed violence. In W. J. Arnold & M. M. Page, Eds., *Nebraska symposium on motivation*. Lincoln: Univ. of Nebraska Press, 1970. Pp. 95-135. L. Berkowitz & D. A. Knurek. Label-mediated hostility generalization. *Journal of Personality & Social Psychology*, 1969, *13*, 200-6. L. Berkowitz & A. Le-Page. Weapons as aggression-eliciting stimuli. *Journal of Personality & Social Psychology*, 1967, *7*, 202-7.
10. R. R. Sears, E. E. Maccoby, & H. Levin. *Patterns of child-rearing*. Evanston, Ill.: Row, Peterson, 1957.
11. Yarrow, Campbell, & Burton. *Child rearing: An inquiry into research and methods*.
12. A. Bandura. *Aggression: A social learning analysis*. Englewood Cliffs, N.J.: Prentice-Hall, 1973; *Social learning theory*. Morristown, N.J.: General Learning Press, 1971.
13. A. Bandura, D. Ross, & S. A. Ross. Vicarious reinforcement and imitative learning. *Journal of Abnormal & Social Psychology*, 1963, *67*, 601-7. F. B. Steuer, J. M. Applefield, & R. Smith. Televised aggression and the interpersonal aggression of preschool children. *Journal of Experimental Child Psychology*, 1971, *11*, 442-47.

14. W. McCord, J. McCord, & L. K. Zola. *Origins of crime: A new evaluation of the Cambridge-Somerville youth study.* N.Y.: Columbia Univ. Press, 1959. E. Tanay. Psychiatric study of homicide. *American Journal of Psychiatry,* 1969, *125,* 1252-58.

15. L. A. LoSciuto. A national inventory of television viewing behavior and J. Lyle & H. R. Hoffman. Children's use of television and other media. Both in E. A. Rubinstein, G. A. Comstock, & J. P. Murray, Eds., *Television and social behavior.* Vol. 4. Washington, D.C.: U.S. Government Printing Office, 1972.

16. Surgeon General's Advisory Committee on Television and Social Behavior. *Television and growing up: The impact of televised violence.* Washington, D.C.: U.S. Government Printing Office, 1972.

17. R. M. Liebert. Television and social learning: Some relationships between viewing violence and behaving aggressively. In J. P. Murray, E. A. Rubinstein, & G. A. Comstock, Eds., *Television and social behavior.* Washington, D.C.: U.S. Government Printing Office, 1972. Pp. 1-34. See also his more recent book, R. M. Liebert, J. M. Neale, & E. S. Davidson, *The early window: Effects of television on children and youth.* N.Y.: Pergamon, 1973.

18. When radio, motion pictures, and comic books began to rely heavily on violence, research was conducted to determine its effects. See R. C. Peterson & L. L. Thurstone. *Motion pictures and the social attitudes of children.* N.Y.: Macmillan, 1933. F. Thrasher. The comics and delinquency. *Journal of Educational Sociology,* 1949, *23,* 195-205. F. Wertham. *Seduction of the innocent.* N.Y.: Rinehart, 1954.

19. A. Bandura. Influence of model's reinforcement contingencies on the acquisition of imitative responses. *Journal of Personality & Social Psychology,* 1965, *1,* 589-95.

20. D. Bramel, B. Taub, & B. Blum. An observer's reaction to the suffering of his enemy. *Journal of Personality & Social Psychology,* 1968, *8,* 384-92. S. Feshbach. The stimulating versus cathartic effects of a vicarious aggressive activity. *Journal of Abnormal & Social Psychology,* 1961, *63,* 381-85. S. Feshbach & R. Singer. *Television and aggression.* San Francisco: Jossey-Bass, 1971. S. Milgram & R. L. Shotland. *Television and antisocial behavior.* N.Y.: Academic Press, 1973.

21. R. N. Johnson. *Aggression in man and animals.* Philadelphia: Saunders, 1972. P. 159. J. L. Singer. The influence of violence portrayed in television or motion pictures upon overt aggressive behavior. In J. L. Singer, Ed., *The control of aggression and violence.* N.Y.: Academic Press, 1971. Pp. 19-60.

22. J. H. Goldstein, R. L. Rosnow, T. Raday, I. Silverman, & G. D.

Gaskell. Punitiveness in response to films varying in content: A cross-national field study of aggression. *European Journal of Social Psychology,* 5(2), 1975 (forthcoming).

23. S. Chaffee & J. McLeod. Adolescents, parents, and television violence. Paper presented at American Psychological Association, Washington, D.C., 1971.

24. L. Berkowitz. Some aspects of observed aggression. *Journal of Personality & Social Psychology,* 1965, *2,* 359-69. B. M. Wolfe & R. A. Baron. Laboratory aggression related to aggression in naturalistic social situations: Effects of an aggressive model on the behavior of college students and prisoner observers. *Psychonomic Science,* 1971, *24,* 193-94. R. H. Walters & E. L. Thomas. Enhancement of punitiveness by visual and audiovisual displays. *Canadian Journal of Psychology,* 1963, *17,* 244-54.

25. B. H. Kniveton. The effect of rehearsal delay on long-term imitation of filmed aggression. *British Journal of Psychology,* 1973, *64,* 259-65.

26. D. G. Clark & W. B. Blankenburg. Trends in violent content in selected mass media. In G. A. Comstock & E. A. Rubinstein, Eds., *Television and social behavior.* Vol. 1. Washington, D.C.: U.S. Government Printing Office, 1972.

27. Research has indicated that people come to appreciate and value those things to which they are exposed more frequently. R. B. Zajonc. Attitudinal effects of mere exposure. *Journal of Personality & Social Psychology,* 1968, *9* (part 2), 1-27. See also V. B. Cline, R. G. Croft, & S. Courrier. Desensitization of children to television violence. *Journal of Personality & Social Psychology,* 1973, *27,* 360-65.

28. E. O. Boyanowsky, D. Newtson, & E. Walster. Effects of murder on movie preference. *Proceedings, 80th Annual Convention, American Psychological Association,* 1972, *7,* 235-36. Since that time a second study has been called to my attention, in which no particular preference for violent TV shows was found among violent prisoners. E. S. Menzies. Preferences in television content among violent prisoners. *F. C. I. Research Reports,* 1971, *3* (No. 1).

29. J. H. Goldstein. Preference for aggressive movie content; The effects of cognitive salience. Unpublished manuscript, Temple University, Philadelphia, 1972.

30. W. Mischel. *Introduction to personality.* N.Y.: Holt, Rinehart & Winston, 1971.

31. R. J. Barndt & D. M. Johnson. Time orientation in delinquents. *Journal of Abnormal & Social Psychology,* 1955, *51,* 343-45. T. C. Brock & C. DelGuidice. Stealing and temporal orientation. *Journal of Abnormal & Social Psychology,* 1963, *66,* 91-94. L. W. Doob. *Patterning of time.* New Haven: Yale Univ. Press, 1971. Pp. 301-3, 329-31.

D. Kipnis. Studies in character structure. *Journal of Personality & Social Psychology*, 1968, *8*, 217-27. R. C. Marohn, D. Offer, & E. Ostrov. Juvenile delinquents view their impulsivity. *American Journal of Psychiatry*, 1971, *128*, 418-23. A. W. Siegman. The relationship between future time perspective, time estimation, and impulse control in a group of young offenders and in a control group. *Journal of Consulting Psychology*, 1961, *25*, 470-75.

32. R. K. Merton. *Social theory and social structure*. Glencoe, Ill.: Free Press, 1957. Pp. 131-60.

33. A. Bandura & W. Mischel. Modification of self-imposed delay of reward through exposure to live and symbolic models. *Journal of Personality & Social Psychology*, 1965, *2*, 698-705.

34. W. Mischel & E. Staub. Effects of expectancy on working and waiting for larger rewards. *Journal of Personality & Social Psychology*, 1965, *2*, 625-33. J. S. Stumphauzer. Increased delay of gratification in young prison inmates through imitation of high-delay peer models. *Journal of Personality & Social Psychology*, 1972, *21*, 10-17.

35. J. Lever. Soccer: Opium of the Brazilian people. *Trans-Action*, 1969, *7*(2), 36-43.

36. J. H. Crook. The nature and function of territorial aggression. In M. F. A. Montagu, Ed., *Man and aggression*. N.Y.: Oxford Univ. Press, 1968. Pp. 141-78.

37. W. James. The moral equivalent of war. *Memoirs and studies*. London: Longmans, 1911. S. Freud. Civilization and its discontents. In J. Strachey, Ed., *The standard edition of the complete psychological works of Sigmund Freud*. Vol. 21. London: Hogarth, 1955. R. Ardrey. *The territorial imperative*. N.Y.: Dell, 1966. K. Lorenz. *On aggression*. N.Y.: Harcourt, Brace & World, 1966.

38. A. Storr. *Human aggression*. N.Y.: Atheneum, 1968.

39. J. H. Goldstein & R. L. Arms. Effects of observing athletic contests on hostility. *Sociometry*, 1971, *34*, 83-90.

40. See the more recent studies on sports and aggression by L. Berkowitz & J. T. Alioto. The meaning of an observed event as a determinant of its aggressive consequences. *Journal of Personality & Social Psychology*, 1973, *28*, 206-17. M. M. Lefkowitz, L. O. Walder, L. D. Eron, & L. R. Huesmann. Preference for televised contact sports as related to sex differences in aggression. *Developmental Psychology*, 1973, *9*, 417-20. G. W. Russell. Machiavellianism, locus of control, aggression, performance and precautionary behaviour in ice hockey. *Human Relations*, 1974, *27*, 825-38.

41. Merton. *Social theory and social structure*.

42. The interested reader is directed to J. H. Goldstein & P. E. McGhee, Eds., *The psychology of humor: Theoretical perspectives and em-*

pirical issues. N.Y.: Academic Press, 1972, for a more complete examination of the nature of humor.

43. S. Freud. *Jokes and their relation to the unconscious.* N.Y.: Norton, 1960. (J. Strachey, transl. Original, 1905.) M. Grotjahn. *Beyond laughter.* N.Y.: McGraw-Hill, 1957. W. Mendel. Humor as an index of emotional means. Paper presented at Amer. Assoc. for the Advancement of Science. Philadelphia, December 1971.

44. L. Berkowitz. Aggressive humor as a stimulus to aggressive responses. *Journal of Personality & Social Psychology,* 1970, *16,* 710-17.

45. G. T. Ellis & F. Sekyra III. The effect of aggressive cartoons on the behavior of first grade children. *Journal of Psychology,* 1972, *81,* 37-43. P. Mussen & E. Rutherford. Effects of aggressive cartoons on children's aggressive play. *Journal of Abnormal & Social Psychology,* 1961, *62,* 461-64.

46. It seems that nonhostile humor may serve to reduce subsequent aggression largely by arousing responses which are not compatible with aggression. See R. A. Baron & R. L. Ball. The aggression-inhibiting influence of nonhostile humor. *Journal of Experimental Social Psychology,* 1974, *10,* 23-33.

47. R. L. Coser. Laughter among colleagues. *Psychiatry,* 1960, *23,* 81-95. A. J. Goodrich, J. Henry, & D. W. Goodrich. Laughter in psychiatric staff conferences: A sociopsychiatric analysis. *American Journal of Orthopsychiatry,* 1954, *24,* 175-84. J. D. Goodchilds. On being witty: Causes, correlates, and consequences. In J. H. Goldstein & P. E. McGhee, Eds., *The psychology of humor.* N.Y.: Academic Press, 1972. Pp. 173-93.

48. G. Myrdal. *An American dilemma.* N.Y.: Harper, 1944.

49. A. J. Obrdlik. Gallows humor—A sociological phenomenon. *American Journal of Sociology,* 1942, *47,* 709-16.

50. T. Reik. *Jewish wit.* N.Y.: Gamut Press, 1962.

51. J. H. Goldstein, R. Davis, & D. Herman. The escalation of aggression: Experimental studies. *Journal of Personality & Social Psychology,* 1975, *31,* 162-70.

52. E. S. Dworkin & J. S. Efran. The angered: Their susceptibility to varieties of humor. *Journal of Personality & Social Psychology,* 1967, *6,* 233-36. D. L. Singer. Aggression arousal, hostile humor, catharsis. *Journal of Personality & Social Psychology,* 1968, *8* (1, Part 2). J. F. Strickland. The effects of motivational arousal on humor preferences. *Journal of Abnormal & Social Psychology,* 1959, *57,* 278-81.

53. J. H. Goldstein, J. M. Suls, & S. Anthony. Enjoyment of specific types of humor content: Motivation or salience? In J. H. Goldstein & P. E.

McGhee, Eds., *The psychology of humor.* N.Y.: Academic Press, 1972. Pp. 159-71.
54. S. Anthony, J. H. Goldstein, & J. M. Suls. Humor appreciation: Effects of cognitive schema. Paper presented at Eastern Psychological Association, Washington, D.C., 1973. J. H. Goldstein, A. F. Silverman, & P. Kreiger. A cross-cultural investigation of humor. In press.
55. F. Wertham, *A Sign for Cain.* N.Y.: Warner, 1969.

CHAPTER 3

1. W. Goode. Violence among intimates. In D. J. Mulvihill & M. M. Tumin, Eds., *Crimes of violence.* Washington, D.C.: U.S. Government Printing Office, 1969. Pp. 941-77. Quote from p. 950.
2. See, for example, S. Brier & I. M. Piliavin. Delinquency, situational determinants, and commitment to conformity. *Social Problems,* 1965, *12,* 35-45. N. S. Endler & J. McV. Hunt. S-R inventories of hostility and comparisons of the proportions of variance from persons, responses, and situations for hostility and anxiousness. *Journal of Personality & Social Psychology,* 1968, *9,* 309-15. C. R. Jeffery. *Crime prevention through environmental design.* Beverly Hills: Sage Publications, 1971. S. Milgram. Behavioral study of obedience. *Journal of Abnormal & Social Psychology,* 1963, *67,* 371-78.
3. M. E. Wolfgang. *Patterns in criminal homicide.* Philadelphia: Univ. of Pennsylvania Press, 1958.
4. P. Watson. More "sane" murderers. (London) *Sunday Times,* January 7, 1973.
5. W. D. Connor. Criminal homicide, U.S.S.R./U.S.A.: Reflections on Soviet data in a comparative framework. *Journal of Criminal Law & Criminology,* 1973, *64,* 111-17. J. M. MacDonald. *The murderer and his victim.* Springfield, Ill.: Chas. C. Thomas, 1961. *New York Times,* December 26, 1973, p. 41.
6. R. Clark. *Crime in America.* N.Y.: Simon & Schuster, 1970. M. Amir. *Patterns in forcible rape.* Chicago: Univ. of Chicago Press, 1971.
7. R. A. Berk & H. E. Aldrich. Patterns of vandalism during civil disorders as an indicator of selection of targets. *American Sociological Review,* 1972, *37,* 533-47.
8. J. H. Goldstein, R. Davis, & D. Herman. The escalation of aggression: Experimental studies. *Journal of Personality & Social Psychology,* 1975, *31,* 162-70. B. Latané & J. Darley. *The unresponsive bystander: Why doesn't he help?* N.Y.: Appleton-Century-Crofts, 1970.
9. M. J. Lerner. The desire for justice and reactions to victims. In

J. Macaulay & L. Berkowitz, Eds., *Altruism and helping behavior.*
N.Y.: Academic Press, 1970. Pp. 205-29.

10. C. Jones & E. Aronson. Attribution of fault to a rape victim as a
    function of respectability of the victim. *Journal of Personality & So-
    cial Psychology,* 1973, *26,* 415-19.

11. These figures are for 1968 and come from D. Gil. *Violence against
    children: Physical abuse in the United States.* Cambridge: Harvard
    Univ. Press, 1970.

12. See D. Bakan. *Slaughter of the innocents.* San Francisco: Jossey-
    Bass, 1971.

13. B. F. Steele & C. B. Pollock. A psychiatric study of parents who
    abuse infants and small children. In R. E. Helfer & C. H. Kempe,
    Eds., *The battered child.* Chicago: Univ. of Chicago Press, 1968. Pp.
    103-47. Quote from p. 106.

14. C. H. Kempe, F. N. Silverman, B. F. Steele, W. Droegemueller, &
    H. K. Silver. The battered child syndrome. *Journal of the American
    Medical Association,* 1962, *181,* 17-24.

15. M. G. Morris, R. W. Gould, & P. J. Matthews. Toward prevention of
    child abuse. *Children,* 1964, *11,* 55-60.

16. J. Dollard, L. W. Doob, N. E. Miller, O. H. Mowrer, & R. R. Sears.
    Frustration and aggression. New Haven: Yale Univ. Press, 1939. See
    J. J. Spinetta & D. Rigler. The child-abusing parent: A psychological
    review. *Psychological Bulletin,* 1972, *77,* 296-304.

17. J. H. Goldstein, R. Davis, & D. Herman. The escalation of aggres-
    sion. *Journal of Personality & Social Psychology.*

18. S. Milgram. Some conditions of obedience and disobedience to au-
    thority. *Human Relations,* 1965, *18,* 57-75. P. G. Zimbardo. The hu-
    man choice: Individuation, reason and order versus deindividuation,
    impulse and chaos. In W. J. Arnold & D. Levine, Eds., *Nebraska
    symposium on motivation.* Lincoln: Univ. of Nebraska Press, 1969.
    Pp. 237-309.

19. P. H. Tannenbaum. Studies in film- and television-mediated arousal
    and aggression: A progress report. In G. Comstock, E. Rubinstein, &
    J. Murray, Eds., *Television and social behavior.* Vol. 5. Washington,
    D.C.: U.S. Government Printing Office, 1971.

20. E. C. O'Neal & L. Kaufman. The influence of attack, arousal and in-
    formation about one's arousal upon interpersonal aggression. *Psy-
    chonomic Science,* 1972, *26,* 211-14.

21. A. M. Barclay & R. N. Haber. The relation of aggressive to sexual
    motivation. *Journal of Personality,* 1965, *33,* 462-75. L. Berkowitz.
    Sex and violence: We can't have it both ways. *Psychology Today,*
    1971, *5* (7), 14 ff. J. H. Goldstein, R. L. Rosnow, T. Raday, I. Silver-

man, & G. D. Gaskell. Punitiveness in response to films varying in content: A cross-national field study of aggression. *European Journal of Social Psychology.* In press. D. Zillmann. Excitation transfer in communication-mediated aggressive behavior. *Journal of Experimental Social Psychology,* 1971, *7,* 419-34.

22. L. Berkowitz. Repeated frustrations and expectations in hostility arousal. *Journal of Abnormal & Social Psychology,* 1960, *60,* 422-29. A. H. Buss. Physical aggression in relation to different frustrations. *Journal of Abnormal & Social Psychology,* 1963, *67,* 1-7. I. Feierabend & R. Feierabend. Aggressive behavior within polities, 1948-1962: A cross-national study. *Journal of Conflict Resolution,* 1966, *10,* 249-71.

23. R. G. Geen & E. C. O'Neal. Activation of cue-elicited aggression by general arousal. *Journal of Personality & Social Psychology,* 1969, *11,* 289-92.

24. A. M. Barclay. Linking sexual and aggressive motives: Contributions of "irrelevant" arousals. *Journal of Personality,* 1971, *39,* 481-92. It should be mentioned that research subjects in many of these studies were required by the experimenter to act aggressively. There has been no research on whether sexually aroused persons show an increased *desire* to behave aggressively. It should also be pointed out that those who have committed violence may be more easily aroused by the environment than nonviolent persons. See G. A. Kercher & C. E. Walker. Reactions of convicted rapists to sexually explicit stimuli. *Journal of Abnormal Psychology,* 1973, *81,* 46-50; and F. Farley & S. Farley. Stimulus-seeking motivation and delinquent behavior among institutionalized delinquent girls. *Journal of Consulting & Clinical Psychology,* 1972, *39,* 94-97.

25. S. Feshbach. Sex and aggression: Some theoretical issues and empirical research. Unpublished manuscript, Univ. of California, Los Angeles, 1973. A. Freud. Comments on aggression. *International Journal of Psychoanalysis,* 1972, *53,* 163-71. K. E. Moyer. *The physiology of hostility.* Chicago: Markham, 1971.

26. J. B. Calhoun. Population density and social pathology. *Scientific American,* 1962, *206,* 139-48.

27. Federal Bureau of Investigation. Uniform Crime Reports, 1971.

28. J. L. Freedman, A. S. Levy, R. W. Buchanan, & J. M. Price. Crowding and human aggressiveness. *Journal of Experimental Social Psychology,* 1972, *8,* 528-48. G. M. Carstairs. Overcrowding and human aggression. In H. D. Graham & T. R. Gurr, Eds., *The history of violence in America.* N.Y.: Bantam, 1969. P. Draper. Crowding among hunter-gatherers: The !kung bushmen. *Science,* 1973, *182,* 301-3.

L. Weiss & M. O'Sullivan. Crowding, noise and measures of human aggression. Paper presented at Western Psychological Association, Anaheim, Calif., 1973.

29. P. G. Zimbardo. The human choice. *Nebraska symposium on motivation.* E. Diener, K. L. Westford, C. Diener, & A. L. Beaman. Deindividuating effects of group presence and arousal on stealing by Halloween trick-or-treaters. *Proceedings, 81st Annual Convention, A.P.A., 1973, 8,* 219-20. H. E. Ransford. Isolation, powerlessness, and violence: A study of attitudes and participation in the Watts riot. *American Journal of Sociology,* 1968, *73,* 581-91. R. I. Watson, Jr. Investigation into deindividuation using a cross-cultural survey technique. *Journal of Personality & Social Psychology,* 1973, *25,* 342-45.

30. *New York Post.* November 26, 1971.

31. R. A. Baron. Aggression as a function of ambient temperature and prior anger arousal. *Journal of Personality & Social Psychology,* 1972, *21,* 183-89. W. Griffitt. Environmental effects on interpersonal affective behavior: Ambient effective temperature and attraction. *Journal of Personality & Social Psychology,* 1970, *15,* 240-44. W. Griffitt & R. Veitch. Hot and crowded: Influences of population density and temperature on interpersonal affective behavior. *Journal of Personality & Social Psychology,* 1971, *17,* 92-98.

32. R. A. Baron & S. F. Lawton. Environmental influences on aggression: The facilitation of modeling effects by high ambient temperatures. *Psychonomic Science,* 1972, *26,* 80-82.

33. R. D. Gastil. Homicide and a regional culture of violence. *American Sociological Review,* 1971, *36,* 412-27.

34. See P. Bohannan. *African homicide and suicide.* Princeton: Princeton Univ. Press, 1960, in which it is shown that the homicide rate for African blacks is considerably lower than the rate for American whites. Hence the conclusion that violence is somehow a racial matter must be rejected.

35. M. E. Wolfgang. *Patterns in criminal homicide.* Pp. 143-67. See also W. C. Reckless. *American criminology: New directions.* N.Y.: Appleton-Century-Crofts, 1973. Pp. 16-17.

36. L. M. Shupe. Alcohol and crime: A study of the urine alcohol concentration found in 882 persons arrested during or immediately after the commission of a felony. *Journal of Criminal Law & Criminology,* 1954, *44,* 661-64.

37. R. M. Bennett, A. H. Buss, & J. A. Carpenter. Alcohol and human physical aggression. *Quarterly Journal of Studies on Alcohol,* 1969, *30,* 870-76.

38. R. J. Shuntich & S. P. Taylor. The effects of alcohol on human physi-

cal aggression. *Journal of Experimental Research in Personality*, 1972, *6*, 34-38.

39. R. B. Carroll. Analysis of alcoholic beverages by gas-liquid chromatography. *Quarterly Journal of Studies on Alcohol*, 1970, Supplement 5, 6-19.

40. A. I. Teger, E. S. Katkin, & D. G. Pruitt. Effects of alcoholic beverages and their congener content on level and style of risk taking. *Journal of Personality & Social Psychology*, 1969, *11*, 170-76. J. Cohen. *Chance, skill and luck, the psychology of guessing and gambling*. Baltimore: Penguin, 1960. R. S. Ryback & D. Ingle. Effect of ethanol and bourbon on Y-maze learning and shock avoidance in the goldfish. *Quarterly Journal of Studies on Alcohol*, 1970, Supplement 5, 136-41.

41. P. E. Nathan, N. C. Zare, E. W. Ferneau, Jr., & L. M. Lowenstein. Effects of congener differences in alcoholic beverages on the behavior of alcoholics. *Quarterly Journal of Studies on Alcohol*, 1970, Supplement 5, 87-100.

42. H. V. Peeke, G. E. Ellman & M. J. Herz. Dose dependent alcohol effects on the aggressive behavior of the convict cichlid (Cichlasoma Nigrofasciatum). *Behavioral Biology*, 1973, *8*, 115-22. Also see D. C. Glass & J. L. Singer. *Urban stress*. N.Y.: Academic Press, 1972.

43. H. S. Becker. Becoming a marijuana user. *American Journal of Sociology*, 1953, *59*, 235-42. Also see S. Schachter. *Emotion, obesity and crime*. N.Y.: Academic Press, 1971.

44. J. R. Tinklenberg & R. C. Stillman. Drug use and violence. In D. N. Daniels, M. F. Gilula, & F. M. Ochberg, Eds., *Violence and the struggle for existence*. Boston: Little, Brown, 1970. Pp. 327-65.

45. A. R. Makadon. The case for free heroin. *Philadelphia Inquirer Magazine*, December 5, 1971.

46. M. S. Eisenhower. Introduction and overview. In H. D. Graham, Ed., *Violence: The crisis of American confidence*. Baltimore: Johns Hopkins Press, 1971. Pp. xv-xxx.

47. National Commission on the Causes & Prevention of Violence. Commission statement on firearms and violence, July 28, 1969.

48. N. Morris & G. Hawkins. *The honest politician's guide to crime control*. Chicago: Univ. of Chicago Press, 1970. P. 65.

49. L. Berkowitz & A. LePage. Weapons as aggression-eliciting stimuli. *Journal of Personality & Social Psychology*, 1967, *7*, 202-7.

50. This finding has not been replicated in several attempts. A. H. Buss, A. Booker, & E. Buss. Firing a weapon and aggression. *Journal of Personality & Social Psychology*, 1972, *22*, 296-302. D. P. Ellis,

P. Weinir, & L. Miller III. Does the trigger pull the finger? An experimental test of weapons as aggression-eliciting stimuli. *Sociometry,* 1971, *34,* 453-65. M. M. Page & R. J. Scheidt. The elusive weapons effect: Demand awareness, evaluation apprehension, and slightly sophisticated subjects. *Journal of Personality & Social Psychology,* 1971, *20,* 304-18.

51. L. Berkowitz. Impulse, aggression and the gun. *Psychology Today,* September 18-22, 1960.

52. M. Harrison & A. Pepitone. Contrast effect in the use of punishment. *Journal of Personality & Social Psychology,* 1972, *23,* 398-404.

53. N. Morris & G. Hawkins. *The honest politician's guide to crime control.* P. 67.

54. J. Jacobs. *The death and life of great American cities.* N.Y.: Random House, 1961. C. R. Jeffery. *Crime prevention through environmental design.* C. R. Jeffery. Environmental design and the prevention of behavioral disorders and criminality. Paper presented at Centre of Criminology, Univ. of Toronto, January 25, 1973. O. Newman. *Defensible space.* N.Y.: Macmillan, 1972.

55. P. David & J. Scott. A cross-cultural comparison of juvenile offenders, offenses, due process, and societies. *Criminology,* 1973, *11,* 183-205.

56. W. L. Yancey. Architecture, interaction, and social control: The case of a large scale housing project. In J. Wohlwill & D. Carson, Eds., *Environment and the social sciences.* Washington, D.C.: American Psychological Assoc., 1972. Pp. 126-35.

CHAPTER 4

1. H. Spencer. *Essays.* N.Y.: Appleton, 1910.

2. M. D. Blumenthal, R. L. Kahn, F. M. Andrews, & K. B. Head. *Justifying violence: Attitudes of American men.* Ann Arbor, Mich.: Institute for Social Research, 1972.

3. *New York Times.* November 26, 1973.

4. R. H. Walters & L. Demkow. Timing of punishment as a determinant of response inhibition. *Child Development,* 1963, *34,* 207-14.

5. Uniform Crime Reports. F.B.I.: Washington, D.C., 1971.

6. Some biopsychologists have argued that sex differences in aggression are due largely to hormonal differences between boys and girls, particularly during adolescence. See K. E. Moyer, *The physiology of hostility.* Chicago: Markham, 1971.

7. Uniform Crime Reports. 1971. P. 34.

8. M. D. Blumenthal, R. L. Kahn, F. M. Andrews, & K. B. Head. *Justi-*

fying violence: Attitudes of American men. Quote from pages 132-33.
9. M. L. Hoffman. Moral development. In P. H. Mussen, Ed., *Carmichael's manual of child psychology.* Vol. 2. N.Y.: Wiley, 1970. Pp. 261-359.
10. J. Aronfreed. *Conduct and conscience: The socialization of internalized control over behavior.* N.Y.: Academic Press, 1968.
11. J. Piaget. *The moral judgment of the child.* N.Y.: Harcourt, Brace, 1932. L. Kohlberg. Moral development and identification. In H. W. Stevenson, Ed., *Child psychology: 62nd yearbook of the National Society for the Study of Education.* Chicago: Univ. of Chicago Press, 1963.
12. E. Staub. The learning and unlearning of aggression: The role of anxiety, empathy, efficacy, and prosocial values. In J. L. Singer, Ed., *The control of aggression and violence.* N.Y.: Academic Press, 1971. Pp. 93-124.
13. W. Hudgins & N. M. Prentice. Moral judgment in delinquent and nondelinquent adolescents and their mothers. *Journal of Abnormal Psychology,* 1973, *82,* 145-52.
14. A. Rapoport. *Fights, games, and debates.* Ann Arbor: Univ. of Michigan Press, 1960.
15. E. E. Maccoby. The development of moral values and behavior in childhood. In J. A. Clausen, Ed., *Socialization and society.* Boston: Little, Brown, 1968. Pp. 227-69. Quote from p. 256.
16. L. Berkowitz. The self, selfishness and altruism. In J. Macaulay & L. Berkowitz, Eds., *Altruism and helping behavior.* N.Y.: Academic Press, 1970. Pp. 143-51.
17. J. Fishkin, K. Keniston, & C. MacKinnon. Moral reasoning and political ideology. *Journal of Personality & Social Psychology,* 1973, *27,* 109-19.
18. Kohlberg. Moral development and identification.
19. Hudgins & Prentice. Moral judgment in delinquent and nondelinquent adolescents and their mothers.
20. See U. G. Foa & E. B. Foa. *Societal structures of the mind.* Springfield, Ill.: Chas. C. Thomas, 1974.
21. L. B. Murphy. *Social behavior and child personality: An exploratory study of some roots of sympathy.* N.Y.: Columbia Univ. Press, 1937.
22. A negative correlation was found between peoples' level of hostility and the amount of money which they were willing to donate to charity, in a study by J. H. Goldstein, R. L. Rosnow, T. Raday, I. Silverman, & G. D. Gaskell. Punitiveness in response to films varying in content: A cross-national field study of aggression. *European Journal of Social Psychology,* in press.
23. J. Macaulay & L. Berkowitz, Eds., *Altruism and helping behavior.*

N.Y.: Academic Press, 1970. L. G. Wispé, Ed., Positive forms of social behavior. *Journal of Social Issues*, 1973, *28*, No. 3.

24. L. G. Wispé. Positive forms of social behavior: An overview. In L. G. Wispé, Ed., Positive forms of social behavior. *Journal of Social Issues*, 1973, *28*, No. 3, 1-19.

25. H. A. Hornstein. Promotive tension: The basis of prosocial behavior from a Lewinian perspective. In L. G. Wispé, Ed., Positive forms of social behavior. *Journal of Social Issues*, 1973, *28*, No. 3, 191-218.

26. P. G. Zimbardo. The human choice: Individuation, reason and order versus deindividuation, impulse and chaos. In W. J. Arnold & D. Levine, Eds., *Nebraska Symposium on Motivation*, 1969, *17*, 237-307. L. Festinger, A. Pepitone, & T. Newcomb. Some consequences of deindividuation in a group. *Journal of Abnormal & Social Psychology*, 1952, *47*, 382-89.

27. E. Staub. *The development of prosocial behavior in children.* Morristown, N.J.: General Learning Press, 1975.

28. P. London. The rescuers: Motivational hypotheses about Christians who saved Jews from the Nazis. In J. Macaulay & L. Berkowitz, Eds., *Altruism and helping behavior*. N.Y.: Academic Press, 1970. Pp. 241-50. Quote from p. 248.

29. H. C. Kelman & L. H. Lawrence. Assignment of responsibility in the case of Lt. Calley: Preliminary report on a national survey. *Journal of Social Issues*, 1972, *28*, 177-212. L. Mann. Attitudes toward My Lai and obedience to orders: An Australian survey. *Australian Journal of Psychology*, 1973, *25*, 11-21.

30. *New York Times*, November 11, 1973.

31. J. Aronfreed. The orgins of self-criticism. *Psychological Review*, 1964, *71*, 193-218.

32. See D. J. Bem. Inducing belief in false confessions. *Journal of Personality & Social Psychology*, 1966, *3*, 707-10. And P. G. Zimbardo. The psychology of police confessions. In *Readings in psychology today*. Del Mar, Calif.: CRM, 1970.

33. B. Latané & J. Darley. *The unresponsive bystander: Why doesn't he help?* N.Y.: Appleton-Century-Crofts, 1970. J. H. Goldstein, R. L. Rosnow, T. Raday, I. Silverman, & G. D. Gaskell. Punitiveness in response to films varying in content: A cross-national field study of aggression.

34. O. Newman. *Defensible space: Crime prevention through urban design.* N.Y.: Macmillan, 1972. Quote from p. 100.

35. J. Bryan & M. A. Test. Models and helping: Naturalistic studies in aiding behavior. *Journal of Personality & Social Psychology*, 1967, *6*, 400-7.

36. A. M. Isen. Success, failure, attention and reaction to others: The

warm glow of success. *Journal of Personality & Social Psychology,* 1970, *15,* 294-301. A. M. Isen & P. F. Levin. Effect of feeling good on helping: Cookies and kindness. *Journal of Personality & Social Psychology,* 1972, *21,* 384-88.
37. J. L. Freedman & S. C. Fraser. Compliance without pressure: The foot-in-the-door technique. *Journal of Personality & Social Psychology,* 1966, *4,* 195-202. See also, T. C. Brock. On interpreting the effects of transgression upon compliance. *Psychological Bulletin,* 1969, *72,* 138-45.

CHAPTER 5

1. K. Menninger. *The crime of punishment.* N.Y.: Viking, 1968.
2. A. F. Henry & J. F. Short, Jr. *Suicide and homicide.* N.Y.: Free Press, 1954.
3. I. K. Feierabend & R. L. Feierabend. Aggression behaviors within polities, 1948-1962: A cross-national study. *Journal of Conflict Resolution,* 1966, *10,* 249-71.
4. See, for example, P. B. Horton & G. R. Leslie. *The sociology of social problems.* N.Y.: Appleton-Century-Crofts, 1970. E. M. Shure. *Our criminal society: The social and legal sources of crime in America.* Englewood Cliffs, N.J.: Prentice-Hall, 1969. M. E. Wolfgang & F. Ferracuti. *The subculture of violence.* London: Tavistock, 1967.
5. E. Fromm. *The anatomy of human destructiveness.* N.Y.: Holt, Rinehart & Winston, 1973. Quote from p. 217.
6. National Institute of Mental Health. *Psychosurgery: Perspective on a current problem.* Washington, D.C.: U.S. Government Printing Office, 1973. Greater Boston Medical Committee for Human Rights. *Violence upon the brain.* Boston. Mimeo, undated.
7. See S. Hook. The rights of the victims. *Encounter,* April 1972. Pp. 11-15.
8. J. F. Decker. Curbside deterrence? An analysis of the effect of a slug-rejector device, coin-view window, and warning labels on slug usage in New York City parking meters. *Criminology,* 1972, *10,* 127-42. Quote from page 142.
9. O. Newman. *Defensible space: Crime prevention through urban design.* N.Y.: Macmillan, 1972. Quotes from pages 165-66; 167-69; 174.
10. L. Festinger, S. Schachter, & K. Back. *Social pressures in informal groups: A study of human factors in housing.* Stanford: Stanford Univ. Press, 1950. W. Ittelson & H. Proshansky, Eds. *Environmental psychology.* N.Y.: Holt, Rinehart & Winston, 1972. R. Sommer. *Personal space.* Englewood Cliffs, N.J.: Prentice-Hall, 1969.

11. Newman. *Defensible space.* Pp. 3, 15.
12. President's Commission on Law Enforcement and Administration of Justice. *The challenge of crime in a free society.* N.Y.: Avon, 1968. P. 585.
13. *Philadelphia Inquirer,* March 28, 1971. *New York Post,* November 26, 1971.
14. R. L. Prosterman. *Surviving to 3000: An introduction to the study of lethal conflict.* Belmont, Calif.: Duxbury, 1972. P. 9.
15. See J. S. Campbell. Violence in America. *New York Times Encyclopedic Almanac, 1971.* N.Y.: New York Times, 1970. Pp. 451-52. A. Pinkney. *The American way of violence.* N.Y.: Random House, 1972. E. M. Shure. *Our criminal society.*
16. N. Morris & G. Hawkins. *The honest politician's guide to crime control.* Chicago: Univ. of Chicago Press, 1970. Pp. 63; 65; 66-67.
17. President's Commission on Law Enforcement and Administration of Justice. *The challenge of crime in a free society.*
18. D. L. Barlett & J. B. Steele. Crime and injustice. *Philadelphia Inquirer* 1973.
19. Campbell. Violence in America.
20. R. Clark. *Crime in America.* N.Y.: Simon & Schuster, 1970. P. 33.
21. There are a number of studies on legal sanctions and crime, most of which show a negligible correlation between the two. W. C. Bailey & R. W. Smith. Punishment: Its severity and certainty. *Journal of Criminal Law, Criminology and Police Science,* 1972, *63,* 530-39. W. J. Chambliss. The deterrent influence of punishment. *Crime & Delinquency,* 1966, *12,* 70-75. T. Sellin. Homicides in retentionist and abolitionist states. In T. Sellin, Ed., *Capital punishment.* N.Y.: Harper & Row, 1967. Pp. 135-38. C. R. Tittle. Crime rates and legal sanctions. *Social Problems,* 1969, *16,* 409-23.
22. R. Clark. *Crime in America.* President's Commission on Law Enforcement & Administration of Justice. *The challenge of crime in a free society.* P. 270.
23. J. Mitford. *Kind and usual punishment: The prison business.* N.Y.: Knopf, 1973. P. 64.
24. N. Morris & G. Hawkins. *The honest politician's guide to crime control.* P. 5.
25. From a study by H. Ruth, reported in J. M. Markham. Heroin hunger does not a mugger make. *N.Y. Times Magazine,* March 18, 1973.
26. President's Commission on Law Enforcement and Administration of Justice. *The challenge of crime in a free society.* P. 510.
27. T. J. Stachnik. The case against criminal penalties for illicit drug use. *American Psychologist,* 1972, *27,* 637-42. Quote from p. 639.

28. S. Lessard. Busting our mental blocks on drugs and crime. *The Washington Monthly,* June 1971, *3,* 6-18.
29. T. J. Stachnik. The case against criminal penalties for illicit drug use. P. 642.
30. President's Commission on Law Enforcement and Administration of Justice. *The challenge of crime in a free society.* Pp. 653-55.
31. National Commission on the Causes and Prevention of Violence. *To establish justice, to insure domestic tranquility.* National Advisory Commission on Civil Disorders. *Report to the National Advisory Commission on Civil Disorders.* N.Y.: Bantam, 1968.
32. President's Commission on Law Enforcement and Administration of Justice. *The challenge of crime in a free society.* Pp. 655-57.
33. M. P. Pines. An answer to the problem of bail: A proposal in need of empirical confirmation. *Columbia Journal of Law and Social Problems,* 1973, *9,* 394-441.
34. Mitford. *Kind and usual punishment.* P. 76.
35. President's Commission on Law Enforcement and Administration of Justice. *The challenge of crime in a free society.* P. 349.
36. C. Haney, C. Banks, & P. Zimbardo. Interpersonal dynamics in a simulated prison. *International Journal of Criminology & Penology,* 1973, *1,* 69-97.
37. Menninger. *The crime of punishment.* P. 65.
38. See A. Bandura. *Aggression: A social-learning analysis.* Englewood Cliffs, N.J.: Prentice-Hall, 1973. Pp. 313-14.
39. Board of Directors. National Council on Crime and Delinquency. The nondangerous offender should not be imprisoned: A policy statement. *Crime and Delinquency,* 1973, *19,* 449-56.
40. Mitford. *Kind and usual punishment.* P. 285.
41. M. J. Chandler. Egocentrism and antisocial behavior: The assessment and training of social perspective-taking skills. *Developmental Psychology,* 1973, *9,* 326-32.
42. J. F. Alexander & B. V. Parsons. Short-term behavioral intervention with delinquent families: Impact on family process and recidivism. *Journal of Abnormal Psychology,* 1973, *81,* 219-25. Quote from p. 224.
43. T. M. Ostrom, C. M. Steele, L. K. Rosenblood, & H. L. Mirels. Modification of delinquent behavior. *Journal of Applied Social Psychology,* 1971, *1,* 118-36. Quote from p. 119.
44. R. P. Hawkins, R. F. Peterson, E. Schweid & S. W. Bijou. Behavior therapy in the home: Amelioration of problem parent-child relations with the parent in a therapeutic role. *Journal of Experimental Child Psychology,* 1966, *4,* 99-107. G. R. Patterson, J. A. Cobb, & R. S.

Ray. A social engineering technology for retraining the families of aggressive boys. In H. Adams & I. Unikel, Eds., *Issues and trends in behavior therapy*. Springfield, Ill.: Chas. C. Thomas, 1973.

CHAPTER 6

1. A. Pinkney. *The American way of violence*. N.Y.: Random House, 1972. P. 164.
2. President's Commission on Law Enforcement and Administration of Justice. *The challenge of crime in a free society*. N.Y.: Avon, 1968. National Advisory Commission on Civil Disorders. *Report of the national advisory commission on civil disorders*. N.Y.: Bantam, 1968. National Commission on the Causes and Prevention of Violence. *To establish justice, to insure domestic tranquility*. N.Y.: Bantam, 1970.
3. See L. A. Coser. Some social functions of violence. *Annals of the American Academy of Political & Social Science*, 1966, *364*, 8-18. E. S. Shneidman & N. L. Farberow. *Clues to suicide*. N.Y.: McGraw-Hill, 1957.
4. President's Commission on Law Enforcement and Administration of Justice. *The challenge of crime in a free society*. P. 642.
5. National Commission on the Causes and Prevention of Violence. *To establish justice, to insure domestic tranquility*. P. 58.
6. See S. Brier & I. M. Piliavin. Delinquency, situational determinants, and commitment to conformity. *Social Problems*, 1965, *12*, 35-45. I. M. Piliavin, J. A. Hardyck, & A. C. Vadum. Constraining effects of personal costs on the transgressions of juveniles. *Journal of Personality & Social Psychology*, 1968, *10*, 227-31.
7. U. Bronfenbrenner. *Two worlds of childhood: U.S. and U.S.S.R.* N.Y.: Russell Sage Foundation, 1970.
8. N. Sanford. Going beyond prevention. In N. Sanford & C. Comstock, Eds., *Sanctions for evil*. San Francisco: Jossey-Bass, 1971. Quote from pp. 316-17.
9. L. Berkowitz & J. Macaulay. The contagion of criminal violence. *Sociometry*, 1971, *34*, 328-60.
10. D. E. Payne & K. P. Payne. Newspapers and crime in Detroit. *Journalism Quarterly*, 1970, *47*, 233-38.
11. T. C. Brock. Implications of commodity theory for value change. In A. G. Greenwald, T. C. Brock, & T. M. Ostrom, Eds., *Psychological foundations of attitudes*. N.Y.: Academic Press, 1968. Pp. 243-75. H. L. Fromkin & T. C. Brock. Erotic materials: A commodity theory analysis of the enhanced desirability that may accompany their unavailability. *Journal of Applied Social Psychology*, 1973, *3*, 219-31.

12. National Commission on the Causes and Prevention of Violence. Pp. 172-73.
13. *TV Guide.* January 5-11, 1974, p. A-1.
14. N. Johnson. *How to talk back to your television set.* Boston: Little, Brown, 1967.
15. R. A. Baron. Reducing the influence of an aggressive model. *Journal of Personality & Social Psychology,* 1971, *20,* 240-45. J. Bryan & M. Test. Models and helping: Naturalistic studies in aiding behavior. *Journal of Personality & Social Psychology,* 1967, *6,* 400-7. L. J. Holper, J. H. Goldstein, & P. Snyderman. The placement of neutral stimulus material in reducing the impact of aggression in the mass media. *Representative Research in Social Psychology,* 1973, *4,* 28-35.
16. I. L. Janis. Groupthink among policy makers. In N. Sanford & C. Comstock, Eds., *Sanctions for evil.* Pp. 71-89. Quote from pp. 73-74.
17. *Philadelphia Inquirer,* August 4, 1973, *Evening Bulletin,* August 4, 1973, *New York Times,* August 5, 1973.
18. H. A. Bloch & G. Geis. *Man, crime, and society.* N.Y.: Random House, 1962. Quote from p. 383.
19. E. H. Sutherland. *White collar crime.* N.Y.: Holt, Rinehart & Winston, 1949.
20. T. Coffin. *The armed society: Militarism in modern America.* Baltimore: Penguin, 1964. Quote from p. 13.
21. National Commission on the Causes & Prevention of Violence. P. xxxvi.
22. F. Wertham. *A sign for Cain.* N.Y.: Warner, 1969. P. 127.
23. M. Deutsch. Psychological alternatives to war. *Journal of Social Issues,* 1962, *18,* 97-119. H. C. Kelman, Ed. *International behavior: A social-psychological analysis.* N.Y.: Holt, Rinehart & Winston, 1965. C. E. Osgood. *An alternative to war or surrender.* Urbana: Univ. of Illinois Press, 1965. M. Sherif. Superordinate goals in the reduction of intergroup conflict. *American Journal of Sociology,* 1958, *63,* 349-56.
24. J. Irwin. *The felon.* Englewood Cliffs, N.J.: Prentice-Hall, 1970. P. 204.
25. See D. T. Campbell. Reforms as experiments. *American Psychologist,* 1969, *24,* 409-29.

NAME INDEX

SUBJECT INDEX

Adrenalin, 75
Aggressible environments, 21, 139
Aggression: definition of, x-xi; in
  animals, 4-8; and genetics, 4,
  8-9, 18; instinct and, 4-11, 13,
  14, 41; preference for, 43;
  theories of, 14, 15, 16; typol-
  ogies, 15-17. *See also* Humor;
  Juvenile delinquency; Victims
Aggression conflict, 19, 23-24, 66,
  68, 72, 87-88, 107
Aggressive humor. *See* Humor
Alcohol, 63-64, 78-81
Alcoholism, 131
Alienation, 13, 23, 103, 110
Altruism. *See* Prosocial behavior
Angry aggression, 15
Anomie. *See* Alienation
Anxiety, 56, 91, 94, 102
Arapesh, 12
Architectural design, 84, 103, 114.
  See also Environmental factors
Argentina, 84
Arousal, 41, 75, 79, 86; sexual, 56,
  75
Assault, 26, 84
Attitudes: toward agggression, 19,
  20, 92-93; toward law, police,
  29, 132, 134-39. *See also* Norms

Australia, 83, 101, 120
Austria, 120
Auto theft, 81, 84, 118

Bail, 125, 136
Baltimore, 119, 120
Battered child syndrome. *See* Child
  abuse
Belgium, 83
Boxing, 40, 47
Brain stimulation, 6-8, 18
Burglary, 84

Canada, 83, 120
Catharsis, 36, 48, 50, 53, 55, 164
Censorship, 151
Central nervous system, 80
Child abuse, 26, 70-75, 148-49
Child-rearing, 29, 61, 99-100, 121,
  147. *See also* Socialization
Civil disobedience, 145
Classical conditioning, 27, 146
Cognitive dissonance, 165
Cognitive factors and aggression,
  7, 18, 23, 46, 68-70, 96, 112
Congeners. *See* Alcohol
Courts, 136-37

Crime, 37, 67; statistics, 76. *See
    also* specific crimes
Crowding and aggression, 76-77
Culture and aggression, 11, 12

Death instinct, 9
Deindividuation, 99, 139
Delay of gratification. *See* Im-
    pulsivity
Denmark, 83, 119
Detroit, 151
Displaced aggression, 16
Drugs, 78-81, 131. *See also* specific
    drugs

Electrical stimulation of the brain.
    See Brain stimulation
England, 78, 83, 119, 121
Environmental factors and aggres-
    sion, 62-63, 67, 84-85; crime
    control and, 112-19. *See also*
    Situational variables
Escalation of aggression, 72-75

Familiarity and aggression, 41, 65-
    67. *See also* Victim-offender re-
    lations
F.B.I. Uniform Crime Reports,
    130, 131, 155, 156
Fear. *See* Anxiety
Finland, 120
Fixed action pattern, 14
Football, 40, 46, 48, 49-51
France, 83, 120
Frustration, 50, 64, 75
Frustration-aggression theory, 16,
    48, 71

Genetics and aggression, 4, 8-9, 18
Greece, 120
Guns, 81, 83; control of, 82, 119-
    123. *See also* Weapons

Heroin, 81; addiction, 85, 132-34
Hockey, 47
Homicide, 26, 43, 62-64, 77, 82,
    83, 109, 119, 120, 123; motives
    for, 62; and alcohol, 63-64

Hong Kong, 120
Hostility, 49-51, 97
Humor: hostile, 52-59, 75
Hungary, 120

Imitation, 20, 28, 30, 44-46, 106,
    127, 146. *See also* Social learn-
    ing theory
Impulsivity, 44-46, 67, 68, 77, 90,
    95, 96, 112, 139
Inhibition, 9, 19, 21, 67, 81
Ireland, 83, 120
Israel, 120
Italy, 12, 77, 83, 120

Japan, 83, 120
"Just world phenomenon," 69-70,
    97
Juvenile delinquency, 17, 97, 119,
    140-43

Kansas City, 102
Kwakiutl, 11

Law of effect, 126
Learning theories, 15, 29-30. *See
    also* Social learning theory
Lepchas, 12
Life instinct, 9, 13
Liverpool, 119, 120
London, 119
Looting, 65

Marihuana, 80, 81
Mass media, 26, 31, 32-43, 47, 120,
    127, 150-54
Mexico, 83
Militarism, 157-59
Modal level of aggression, 26, 27,
    51, 60, 61
Models. *See* Social learning theory
Moral development, 93-97, 148,
    149
Murder. *See* Homicide
My Lai, 101

Netherlands, 120
New York City, 77, 119

Victim-offender relations, 62-63,
   65-75
Victimless crimes, 130-34
Vietnam War, 4, 12, 55, 58, 153,
   157

Weapons, 26, 29, 65, 78, 81-83, 86,

   119-23, 146; toy, 40; *See also*
   Guns
West Germany, 120
White collar crime, 155

XYY syndrome, 8-9, 18

Yugoslavia, 78